Baby Doll and Other Plays

Tennessee Williams was born in 1911 in Columbus, Mississippi, where his grandfather was the episcopal clergyman. When his father, a travelling salesman, moved with his family to St Louis some years later, both he and his sister found it impossible to settle down to city life. He entered college during the Depression and left after a couple of years to take a clerical job in a shoe company. He stayed there for two years, spending the evenings writing. He entered the University of Iowa in 1938 and completed his course, at the same time holding a number of part-time jobs of great diversity. He received a Rockefeller Fellowship in 1940 for his play *Battle of Angels*, and he won the Pulitzer Prize in 1948 and 1955. Among his many other plays Penguin have published *The Rose Tattoo* (1951), *Camino Real* (1953), *Cat on a Hot Tin Roof* (1955), *Orpheus Descending* (1957), *Suddenly Last Summer* (1958), *Period of Adjustment* (1960), *The Night of the Iguana* (1961), *The Milk Train Doesn't Stop Here Anymore* (1963), and *Small Craft Warning* (1972). Tennessee Williams died in 1983.

Peter Shaffer has written of Tennessee Williams: 'He was a born dramatist as few are ever born. Whatever he put on paper, superb or superfluous, glorious or gaudy, could not fail to be electrifyingly actable. He could not write a dull scene . . . Tennessee Williams will live as long as drama itself.'

D1637569

TENNESSEE WILLIAMS

Baby Doll
THE SCRIPT FOR THE FILM
Something Unspoken
Summer and Smoke

PENGUIN BOOKS

PENGUIN CLASSICS

Published by the Penguin Group
Penguin Books Ltd, 80 Strand, London WC2R ORL, England
Penguin Group (USA) Inc., 375 Hudson Street, New York, New York 10014, USA
Penguin Group (Canada), 90 Eglinton Avenue East, Suite 700, Toronto, Ontario, Canada M4P 2Y3
(a division of Pearson Penguin Canada Inc.)
Penguin Ireland, 25 St Stephen's Green, Dublin 2, Ireland (a division of Penguin Books Ltd)
Penguin Group (Australia), 250 Camberwell Road, Camberwell, Victoria 3124, Australia
(a division of Pearson Australia Group Pty Ltd)
Penguin Books India Pvt Ltd, 11 Community Centre, Panchsheel Park, New Delhi – 110 017, India
Penguin Group (NZ), 67 Apollo Drive, Rosedale, North Shore 0632, New Zealand
(a division of Pearson New Zealand Ltd)
Penguin Books (South Africa) (Pty) Ltd, 24 Sturdee Avenue,
Rosebank, Johannesburg 2196, South Africa

Penguin Books Ltd, Registered Offices: 80 Strand, London WC2R ORL, England

www.penguin.com

Baby Doll first published in Great Britain by Martin Secker & Warburg Ltd 1957
Something Unspoken first published in Great Britain by Martin Secker & Warburg Ltd 1959
Summer and Smoke first published in Great Britain by Martin Secker & Warburg Ltd 1973
Published in Penguin Classics 2009

2

Baby Doll copyright © 1956, renewed 1984 by The University of the South
Something Unspoken copyright © 1953, renewed 1981 by the University of the South
Summer and Smoke copyright © 1948, renewed 1976 by the University of the South
All rights reserved

Printed in England by Clays Ltd, St Ives plc

ISBN 978-0-141-10029-7

www.greenpenguin.co.uk

Penguin Books is committed to a sustainable future
for our business, our readers and our planet.
The book in your hands is made from paper
certified by the Forest Stewardship Council.

CONTENTS

BABY DOLL

For a number of years Elia Kazan, the director of several of Tennessee Williams' plays on Broadway as well as films, had been urging Mr Williams to weld into an original film story two of his early one-act plays which were, roughly, concerned with the same characters and situation. And in the summer of 1955, while he was travelling in Europe, Mr Williams wrote and dispatched to Mr Kazan a proposed script, quite different from the two short plays. With some changes this was filmed the following winter mainly in the Mississippi rural area which had been the original setting of the two short plays.

Although he had himself adapted several of his Broadway successes for films, this was Mr Williams' first original screen play. Many who came to read it, including his publishers, felt that although few 'shooting' scripts have ever been published, this one was publishable as it stood.

The film, *Baby Doll*, which was previously announced as *The Whip Hand* and *Mississippi Woman*, was produced and directed in the winter of 1955–1956 by Elia Kazan for Newtown Productions, Inc., and is presented by Warner Brothers. The principal roles are filled by Carroll Baker, Eli Wallach, Karl Malden, and Mildred Dunnock.

1]

INTERIOR. DAY.
[*A voluptuous girl, under twenty, is asleep on a bed, with the covers thrown off. This is* BABY DOLL MEIGHAN, ARCHIE LEE'*s virgin wife. A sound is disturbing her sleep, a steady sound, furtive as a mouse scratching, she stirs, it stops, she settles again, it starts again. Then she wakes, without moving, her back to that part of the wall from which the sound comes.*]

2]

INTERIOR. DAY. CLOSE SHOT. BABY DOLL.
[*She is a little frightened of what sounds like a mouse in the woodwork and still doesn't sound like a mouse in the woodwork. Then a crafty look.*]

3]

INTERIOR. DAY. FULL SHOT.
[*She gets up, as the sound is continuing, and moves stealthily out of her room.*]

4]

HALL. DAY. FULL SHOT.
[*She comes out of her room and just as stealthily opens the door to an adjoining room and peeks in.*]

5]

CLOSE SHOT. BABY DOLL.
[*Astonished and angry at what she sees.*]

6]

WHAT SHE SEES. ARCHIE LEE MEIGHAN.
[*He is crouched over a section of broken plaster in the wall, enlarging a space between exposed boards with a penknife. Unshaven, black jowled, in sweaty pyjamas. On the bed table*

behind him is a half-empty bottle of liquor, an old alarm clock, ticking away, a magazine called Spicy Fiction, *and a tube of ointment. After a moment he removes the knife and bends to peer through the enlarged crack.*]

7]

CLOSE SHOT. BABY DOLL.
BABY DOLL: Archie Lee. You're a mess.

8]

ARCHIE LEE.
[*He recovers.*]

9]

BABY DOLL.
BABY DOLL: Y'know what they call such people? Peepin' Toms!

10]

FULL SHOT. ARCHIE LEE'S BEDROOM.
ARCHIE LEE: Come in here, I want to talk to you.
BABY DOLL: I know what you're going to say, but you can save your breath.
ARCHIE LEE: [*Interrupting*] We made an agreement....
BABY DOLL: You promised my daddy that you would leave me alone till I was ready for marriage....
ARCHIE: Well?
BABY DOLL: Well, I'm not ready for it yet....
ARCHIE: And I'm going crazy....
BABY DOLL: Well, you can just wait....
ARCHIE: We made an agreement that when you was twenty years old we could be man and wife in more than just in name only.
BABY DOLL: Well, I won't be twenty till November the seventh....
ARCHIE: Which is the day after tomorrow!

BABY DOLL: How about your side of that agreement – that you'd take good care of me? GOOD CARE OF ME! Do you remember that?! Now the Ideal Pay As You Go Plan Furniture Company is threatening to remove the furniture from this house. And every time I bring that up you walk away. . . .

ARCHIE: Just going to the window to get a breath of air. . . .

BABY DOLL: Now I'm telling you that if the Ideal Pay As You Go Plan Furniture Company takes those five complete sets of furniture out of this house then the understanding between us will be cancelled. Completely!

11]

ARCHIE LEE. AT WINDOW.

[*He is listening. We hear the distant sound of the Syndicate Cotton Gin. Like a gigantic distant throbbing heart-beat.* ARCHIE LEE *puts the window down. He crosses to the mirror, dolefully considers his appearance.*]

BABY DOLL: Yeah, just look at yourself! You're not exactly a young girl's dream come true, Archie Lee Meighan.

[*The phone rings downstairs. This sound is instantly followed by an outcry even higher and shriller.*]

BABY DOLL: Aunt Rose Comfort screams ev'ry time the phone rings.

ARCHIE: What does she do a damn fool thing like that for?

[*The phone rings again.* AUNT ROSE COMFORT *screams downstairs. The scream is followed by high breathless laughter. These sounds are downstairs. Archie Lee exits.*]

BABY DOLL: She says a phone ringing scares her.

12]

HALL.

[ARCHIE *lumbers over to a staircase, much too grand for the present style of the house, and shouts down to the old woman below.*]

ARCHIE: Aunt Rose Comfort, why don't you answer that phone?

13]

DOWNSTAIRS HALL.

[AUNT ROSE *comes out of the kitchen and walks towards the hall telephone, withered hand to her breast.*]

AUNT ROSE: I cain't catch m'breath, Archie Lee. Phone give me such a fright.

ARCHIE: [*From above*] Answer it.

[*She has recovered some now and gingerly lifts the receiver.*]

AUNT ROSE: Hello? This is Miss Rose Comfort McCorkle speaking. No, the lady of the house is Mrs Archie Lee Meighan, who is the daughter of my brother that passed away ...

[ARCHIE LEE *is hurrying down the stairs.*]

ARCHIE: They don't wanta know that! Who in hell is it talking and what do they want?

AUNT ROSE: I'm hard of hearing. Could you speak louder, please? The what? The Ideal Pay As –

[*With amazing, if elephantine, speed,* ARCHIE *snatches the phone from the old woman.*]

ARCHIE: Gi'me that damn phone. An' close the door.

[*The old woman utters her breathless cackle and backs against the door.* ARCHIE *speaks in a hoarse whisper.*]

ARCHIE: Now what is this? Aw. Uh-huh. Today!? Aw. You gotta g'me more time. Yeah, well you see I had a terrible setback in business lately. The Syndicate Plantation built their own cotton gin and're ginnin' out their own cotton, now, so I lost their trade and it's gonna take me a while to recover from that. ...

[*Suddenly*]

Then TAKE IT OUT! TAKE IT OUT! Come and get th' damn stuff. And you'll never get my business again! Never!

[*They have hung up on him. He stands there – a man in tough trouble. Then abruptly starts massaging his exhausted head of hair.*]

AUNT ROSE: [*Timidly*] Archie Lee, honey, you all aren't going to lose your furniture, are you?

ARCHIE: [*Hoarse whisper*] Will you shut up and git on back in the kitchen and don't speak a word that you heard on the phone, if you heard a word, to my wife! And don't holler no more in this house, and don't cackle no more in it either, or by God I'll pack you up and haul you off to th' county home at Sunset.

AUNT ROSE: What did you say, Archie Lee, did you say something to me?

ARCHIE: Yeah. I said shoot. [*He starts upstairs.*]

[AUNT ROSE *cackles uneasily and enters the kitchen. Suddenly, we hear another scream from her. We pan with her, and reveal* OLD FUSSY, *the hen, on top of the kitchen table pecking the corn bread.*]

14]

UPSTAIRS HALL.

[ARCHIE *is heading back to his bedroom.* BABY DOLL *appears in a flimsy wrapper at the turn of the stairs crossing to the bathroom.*]

BABY DOLL: What made her holler this time?

ARCHIE: How in hell would I know what made that ole woman holler this time or last time or the next time she hollers?

BABY DOLL: Last time she hollered it was because you throwed something at her.

[*She enters bathroom.* ARCHIE LEE *stands in doorway.*]

ARCHIE: What did I ever throw at Aunt Rose Comfort?

BABY DOLL: [*From inside bathroom*] Glass a water. Fo' singin' church hymns in the kitchen. . . .

[*We hear the shower go on.*]

ARCHIE: This much water! Barely sprinkled her with it! To catch her attention. She don't hear nothing, you gotta do somethin' to git the ole woman's attention.

[*On an abrupt impulse he suddenly enters the bathroom. Sounds of a struggle. The shower.*]

BABY DOLL: Keep y'r hands off me! Will yuh? Keep your hands off . . . Off.

[ARCHIE LEE *comes out of the bathroom good and wet. The*

shower is turned off. BABY DOLL's *head comes out past the door.*]

BABY DOLL: I'm going to move to the Kotton King Hotel, the very next time you try to break the agreement! The very next time!

[*She disappears. . . .*]

15]

CLOSE SHOT. ARCHIE LEE WET.

DISSOLVE.

16]

ARCHIE LEE.

[*He is seated in his* 1937 *Chevy Sedan. The car is caked with pale-brown mud and much dented. Pasted on the windshield is a photo of* BABY DOLL *smiling with bewilderment at the birdie-in-the-camera.*

ARCHIE LEE *is honking his horn with unconcealed and un-modified impatience.*]

ARCHIE: [*Shouting*] Baby Doll! Come on down here, if you're going into town with me. I got to be at the doctor's in ten minutes. [*No answer*] Baby Doll!!!!

[*From inside the house.* BABY DOLL's *voice.*]

BABY DOLL: If you are so impatient, just go ahead without me. Just go ahead. I know plenty of ways of getting down-town without you.

ARCHIE: You come on.

[*Silence. The sound of the Syndicate Gin.* ARCHIE *does a sort of imitation. His face is violent.*]

ARCHIE: Baby Doll!!!!

[BABY DOLL *comes out on the sagging porch of the mansion. She walks across the loose boards of the porch through stripes of alternate light and shadow from the big porch pillars. She is humming a little cakewalk tune, and she moves in sympathy to it. She has on a skirt and blouse, white, and skintight, and pearl chokers the size of golf balls seen from a medium distance. She draws up beside the car and goes no farther.*]

ARCHIE: You going in town like that?

BABY DOLL: Like what?

ARCHIE: In that there outfit. For a woman of your modest nature that squawks like a hen if her *husband* dast to put his hand on her, you sure do seem to be advertising your –

BABY DOLL: [*Drowning him out*] My figure has filt out a little since I bought my trousseau AND paid for it with m'daddy's insurance money. I got two choices, wear clo'se skintight or go naked, now which do you want me t' –

ARCHIE:

[*Aw, now, hell! Will you git into th' car?*
Their loud angry voices are echoed by the wandering poultry.]

BABY DOLL: I will git into the rear seat of that skatterbolt when you git out of the front seat and walk around here to open the door for me like a gentleman.

ARCHIE: Well, you gonna wait a long time if that's what you're waiting for!

BABY DOLL: I vow my father would turn over in his grave. . . .

ARCHIE: I never once did see your father get out and open a car door for your mother or any other woman. . . . Now get on in. . . .

[*She wheels about and her wedgies clack-clack down the drive.*
At foot of drive she assumes a hitch-hiker's stance. A hot-rod
skids to a sudden and noisy stop. ARCHIE LEE *bounds from his*
car like a jack rabbit, snatching a fistful of gravel as he plummets
down drive. Hurls gravel at grinning teen-age kids in hot-rod,
shouting incoherently as they shoot off, plunging BABY DOLL
and her protector in a dust-cloud. Through the dust . . .]

ARCHIE LEE: Got your licence number you pack a –

DISSOLVE.

16A]

THE CAR INTERIOR.

[*They are jolting down the road.*]

ARCHIE: Baby Doll, y'know they's no torture on earth to equal the torture which a cold woman inflicts on a man that

17

she won't let touch her??!! No torture to compare with it!
What I've done is!! Staked out a lot in hell, a lot with a
rotten house on it and five complete sets of furniture not
paid for. . . .

BABY DOLL: What you done is bit off more'n you can
chew.

ARCHIE: People know the situation between us. Yestiddy on
Front Street a man yelled to me, 'Hey Archie Lee, has
y'wife outgrowed the crib yet??' And three or four others
haw-hawed! Public! Humiliation!

[BABY DOLL *in back seat, her beads and earrings ajingle like a circus pony's harness.*]

BABY DOLL: Private humiliation is just as painful.

ARCHIE: Well! – There's an agreement between us! You
ain't gonna sleep in no crib tomorrow night, Baby, when
we celebrate your birthday.

BABY DOLL: If they remove those five complete sets of
furniture from the house, I sure will sleep in the crib
because the crib's paid for – I'll sleep in the crib or on the
top of Aunt Rose Comfort's pianner. . . .

ARCHIE: And I want to talk to you about Aunt Rose
Comfort. . . . I'm not in a position to feed and keep her
any –

BABY DOLL: Look here, Big Shot, the day Aunt Rose
Comfort is unwelcome under your roof . . .

ARCHIE: Baby Doll, honey, we just got to unload ourselves
of all unnecessary burdens. . . . Now she can't cook and
she –

BABY DOLL: If you don't like Aunt Rose Comfort's cookin',
then get me a regular servant. I'm certainly not going to
cook for a fat ole thing like you, money wouldn't pay me –
Owwwww!

[ARCHIE *has backhanded her. And prepares to do so again.*]

BABY DOLL: Cut that out. . . .

ARCHIE: You better quit saying 'fat ole thing' about me!

BABY DOLL: Well, you get young and thin and I'll quit
calling you a fat old thing. – What's the matter now?

[ARCHIE LEE *points to off right with a heavily tragic gesture.*]

TRAVELLING SHOT. SYNDICATE GIN.
THEIR VIEWPOINT.
> [*It is new, handsome, busy, clearly prospering. A sign (large)
> reads:* SYNDICATE COTTON GIN.]

18]

TWO SHOT. ARCHIE AND BABY DOLL.
ARCHIE: There it is! There it is!
BABY DOLL: Looks like they gonna have a celebration!
ARCHIE: Why shouldn't they!!?? They now got every last
bit of business in the county, including every last bit of
what I used to get.
BABY DOLL: Well, no wonder, they got an up-to-date plant –
not like that big pile of junk you got!!
> [ARCHIE *glares at her.*]

> QUICK DISSOLVE.

19]

WAITING-ROOM. DOCTOR'S OFFICE.
> [ARCHIE *and* BABY DOLL *enter, and he is still hotly pursuing
> the same topic of discussion*.]
ARCHIE: Now I'm just as fond of Aunt Rose Comfort –
BABY DOLL: You ain't just as fond of Aunt –
ARCHIE: Suppose she breaks down on us?? Suppose she gets
a disease that lingers –
> [BABY DOLL *snorts.*]
ARCHIE: All right, but I'm serving you notice. If that ole
woman breaks down and dies on my place, I'm not going
to be stuck with her funeral expenses. I'll have her burned
up, yep, cremated, cremated, is what they call it. And pack
her ashes in an ole Coca-Cola bottle and pitch the bottle
into TIGER TAIL BAYOU!!!
BABY DOLL: [*Crossing to inner door*] Doctor John? Come out
here and take a look at my husband. I think a mad dawg's
bit him. He's gone ravin' crazy!!

RECEPTIONIST: [*Appearing*] Mr Meighan's a little bit late for his appointment, but the doctor will see him.

BABY DOLL: Good! I'm going down to the –

ARCHIE: Oh, no, you're gonna sit here and wait till I come out....

BABY DOLL: Well, maybe ...

[ARCHIE *observes that she is exchanging a long, hard stare with a young man slouched in a chair.*]

ARCHIE: And look at this! Or somethin'.

[*He thrusts a copy of* Screen Secrets *into her hands and shoves her into a chair. Then glares at the young man, who raises his copy of* Confidential.]

DISSOLVE.

20]

INNER OFFICE.

[ARCHIE LEE *has been stripped down to the waist. The doctor has just finished examining him. From the ante-room, laughter, low. Which seems to make* ARCHIE LEE *nervous.*]

DOCTOR: You're not an old man, Archie Lee, but you're not a young man, either.

ARCHIE: That's the truth.

DOCTOR: How long you been married?

ARCHIE: Just about a year now.

DOCTOR: Have you been under a strain? You seem terrible nervous?

ARCHIE: No strain at all! None at all....

[*Sound of low laughter from the waiting-room. Suddenly,* ARCHIE LEE *rushes over and opens the door.* BABY DOLL *and the* YOUNG MAN *are talking. He quickly raises his magazine. ... Archie closes ... the door, finishes dressing....*]

DOCTOR: What I think you need is a harmless sort of sedative....

ARCHIE: Sedative! Sedative! What do I want with a sedative???

[*He bolts out of the office....*]

DISSOLVE.

21]

MEDIUM LONG SHOT. ARCHIE LEE'S CAR
GOING DOWN FRONT STREET.

[BABY DOLL *sits on her side aloof. Suddenly a moving van
passes the other way. On its side is marked the legend,* IDEAL
PAY AS YOU GO PLAN FURNITURE COMPANY. *Suddenly,*
BABY DOLL *jumps up and starts waving her hand, flagging the
van down, then when this fails, flagging* ARCHIE LEE *down.*]

22]

CLOSER SHOT. ARCHIE'S CAR.

BABY DOLL: That was all our stuff!

ARCHIE: No it wasn't. . . .

BABY DOLL: That was our stuff. Turn around, go after them.

ARCHIE: Baby Doll, I've got to wait down here for my per-
scription. . . .

[*At this moment another* IDEAL PAY AS YOU GO PLAN
FURNITURE COMPANY *goes by, in the* OTHER *direction.*]

BABY DOLL: There goes another one, towards our house.

ARCHIE: Baby, let's go catch the show at the Delta Brilliant.

BABY DOLL: [*Starts beating him.*]

ARCHIE: Or let's drive over to the Flaming Pig and have
some barbecue ribs and a little cold beer.

BABY DOLL: That's our stuff . . . !

[ARCHIE LEE *looks the other way.*]

I said that's our stuff . . . !! I wanta go home. HOME. NOW.
If you don't drive me home now, I'll I'll, I'll – Mr Hanna.
Mr Gus Hanna. You live on Tiger Tail Road . . .

ARCHIE: I'll drive you home.

[*He spins the car around and they start home.*]

23]

EXTERIOR MEIGHAN HOUSE. DAY.

[MEIGHAN'S *car turns in the drive. The van we saw is backed
up to the house, and furniture is being removed from the house.*
BABY DOLL *runs among them and starts to beat the movers.*

They go right on with their work, paying no attention. After a time AUNT ROSE *puts her arms around* BABY DOLL *and leads her into the house.*]

24]

CLOSE SHOT. ARCHIE LEE.

[*He really is on a spot. Again he hears the sound of the Syndicate Cotton Gin. He makes the same sound, imitating it, he made earlier. He looks in its direction and spits. Then he gets out of the car and walks towards his empty home.*]

25]

INTERIOR. ARCHIE LEE'S HOUSE.
THE PARLOUR.

[BABY DOLL *is sobbing by the window. The screen door creaks to admit the hulking figure of* ARCHIE LEE.]

ARCHIE: [*Approaching*] Baby Doll. . . .

BABY DOLL: Leave me alone in here. I don't want to sit in the same room with a man that would make me live in a house with no furniture.

ARCHIE: Honey, the old furniture we got left just needs to be spread out a little. . . .

BABY DOLL: My daddy would turn in his grave if he knew, he'd turn in his grave.

ARCHIE: Baby Doll, if your daddy turned in his grave as often as you say he'd turn in his grave, that old man would plough up the graveyard.

[*Somewhere outside* AUNT ROSE *is heard singing; 'Rock of Ages'.*]

ARCHIE: She's out there pickin' roses in the yard just as if nothing at all had happened here. . . .

BABY DOLL: I'm going to move to the Kotton King Hotel. I'm going to move to the Kotton King Hotel. . . .

ARCHIE: No, you ain't, Baby Doll.

BABY DOLL: And I'm going to get me a job. The manager of the Kotton King Hotel carried my daddy's coffin, he'll give me work.

ARCHIE: What sort of work do you think you could do, Baby Doll?

BABY DOLL: I could curl hair in a beauty parlour or polish nails in a barber-shop, I reckon, or I could be a hostess and smile at customers coming into a place.

ARCHIE: What place?

BABY DOLL: Any place! I could be a cashier.

ARCHIE: You can't count change.

BABY DOLL: I could pass out menus or programmes or something and say hello to people coming in! [*Rises*] I'll phone now. [*She exits.*]

26]

HALL.

[BABY DOLL *crosses to the telephone. She is making herself attractive as if preparing for an interview.*]

BABY DOLL: Kotton King? This is Mrs Meighan. I want to reserve a room for tomorrow mornin' and I want to register under my maiden name, which is Baby Doll Carson. My daddy was T. C. Carson who died last summer when I got married and he is a very close personal friend of the manager of the Kotton King Hotel – you know – what's his name. . . .

27]

EXTERIOR OF HOUSE.

[ARCHIE *comes out door and wanders into the yard, passing* AUNT ROSE, *who holds a bunch of roses.*]

AUNT ROSE: Archie Lee, look at these roses! Aren't they poems of nature?

ARCHIE: Uh-huh, poems of nature.

[*He goes past her, through the front gate and over to his Chevy. The front seat on the driver's side has been removed and a broken-down commodious armchair put in its place.*

Sound of the Syndicate Gin, throbbing. ARCHIE LEE *reaches under the chair and fishes out a pint bottle. He takes a slug, listens to the Syndicate, takes another. Then he throws the bottle out of the car, turns the ignition key of the car and ...]*

28]

THE CHEVY ROCKS OUT OF THE YARD.

DISSOLVE.

29]

THE INTERIOR. BRITE SPOT CAFE.

[*A habitually crowded place. Tonight it is empty. In the corner a customer or two. Behind the bar, the man in the white apron with nothing to do is sharpening a frog gig on a stone. Enter* ARCHIE, *goes over to the bar.*]

ARCHIE: Didn't get to the bank today, Billy, so I'm a little short of change....

[*The* BARTENDER *has heard this before. He reaches to a low shelf and takes out an unlabelled bottle and pours* ARCHIE *a jolt.*]

ARCHIE: Thanks. Where's everybody?

BARTENDER: Over to the Syndicate Gin. Free liquor over there tonight. Why don't you go over? [*Then he laughs sardonically.*]

ARCHIE: What's the occasion?

BARTENDER: First anniversary. Why don't you go over and help them celebrate.

ARCHIE: I'm not going to my own funeral either.

BARTENDER: I might as well lock up and go home. All that's coming in here is such as you.

ARCHIE: What you got there?

[*The* BARTENDER *holds up a frog gig. The ends, where just sharpened, glisten.*]

ARCHIE: Been getting any frogs lately?

BARTENDER: Every time I go out. Going tomorrow night and get me a mess. You wanna come? There's a gang going. You look like you could use some fresh meat.

[*Another rather despondent-looking character comes in.*]

ARCHIE: Hey, Mac, how you doing?

MAC: Draggin', man.

BARTENDER: Why ain't you over to the Syndicate like every-body else?

MAC: What the hell would I do over that place... That place ruined me ... ruined me....

BARTENDER: The liquor's running free over there tonight. And they got fireworks and everything....

MAC: Fireworks! I'd like to see the whole place up in smoke.
[*Confidentially*] Say, I'm good for a couple, ain't I?

As the BARTENDER *reaches for the same bottle-without-a-label, we*

DISSOLVE TO

30]

EXTERIOR. SYNDICATE GIN.

[*A big platform has been built for the celebration and decked out with flags, including the Stars and Bars of Dixie and the Mississippi State Banner.*

A band is playing 'Mississippi Millions Love You', the state song, which is being sung by an emotional spinster. Several public officials are present, not all of them happy to be there as the county has a strongly divided attitude towards the Syndicate-owned plantation. Some old local ward heeler is reeling onto the speaker's platform and a signal is given to stop the band music. THE OLD BOY *lifts a tin cup, takes a long swallow and remarks.*]

THE OLD BOY: Strongest branch water that ever wet my whistle. Must of come out of Tiger Tail Bayou.

[*There is a great haw-haw.*]

THE OLD BOY: [*Continues*] Young man? Mr Vacarro. This is a mighty fine party you're throwing tonight to celebrate your first anniversary as superintendent of the Syndicate Plantation and Gin. And I want you to know that all of us good neighbours are proud of your achievement, bringin' in the biggest cotton crop ever picked off the blessed soil of Two River County.

[*The camera has picked up a handsome, cocky young Italian,*

SILVA VACARRO. *His affability is not put on, but he has a way of darting glances right and left as he chuckles and drinks beer which indicates a certain watchfulness, a certain reserve. The camera has also picked up, among the other listeners, some uninvited guests ... including* ARCHIE LEE *and his friend from the Brite Spot.* ARCHIE LEE *is well on the way and, of course, his resentment and bitterness are much more obvious.*]

THE OLD BOY: Now when you first come here, well, we didn't know you yet and some of us old-timers were a little standoffish, at first.

[VACARRO's *face has suddenly gone dark and sober. In his watchfulness he has noticed the hostile guests. With a sharp gesture of his head, he summons a man who works for him —* ROCK — *who comes up and kneels alongside. The following colloquy takes place right through* THE OLD BOY's *lines.*]

SILVA: There's a handful of guys over there that don't look too happy to me. . . .

ROCK: They got no reason to be. You put 'em out of business when you built your own gin, and started to gin your own cotton.

SILVA: Watch 'em, keep an eye on 'em, specially if they start to wander around. . . .

THE OLD BOY: [*Who has continued*] Natchully, a thing that is profitable to some is unprofitable to others. We all know that some people in this county have suffered some financial losses due in some measure to the success of the Syndicate Plantation.

[VACARRO *is looking around again. Rather defiantly, but at no one in particular. Between the knees of his corduroy riding breeches is a whip that he carries habitually, a braided leather riding crop.*]

THE OLD BOY: But as a whole, the community has reaped a very rich profit.

[*He has said this rather defiantly as if he knew he was bucking a certain tide. . . . A voice from the crowd.*]

VOICE: Next time you run for office you better run on the Republican ticket. Git the nigger vote, Fatso!

THE OLD BOY: [*Answering*] Just look at the new construction been going on! Contractors, carpenters, lumbermen, not to mention the owner and proprietor of the Brite Spot down the road there! And not to mention –

[*Suddenly somebody throws something at the speaker, something liquid and sticky. Instantly,* ROCK *and* VACARRO *spring up*. . . .]

ROCK: Who done that?!?!

SILVA: [*Crossing to front of platform*] If anybody's got anything to throw, well, here's your target, here's your standing target! The wop! The foreign wop!!

[*Big rhubarb.* THE OLD BOY *is wiping his face with a wad of paper napkins.*

Suddenly, we see that something in the middle distance is on fire. The wide dark fields begin to light up. Voices cry alarm. Shouts, cries. Everyone and everything is lit by the shaking radiance of the fire.

VACARRO *races towards the fire. It is in the gin building. The volatile dust explodes. Loaded wagons are being pushed away, by Negro field-hands driven by* VACARRO.

A fire engine arrives. But it seems lax in its efforts and inefficient. A hose is pulled out, but there is insufficient water to play water on the blaze, and the hose itself falls short. The firemen are not merely ineffectual. Some seem actually indifferent. In fact, some of their faces express an odd pleasure in the flames, which they seem more interested in watching than fighting.

VACARRO *rushes among them exhorting, commanding, constantly gesturing with his short riding crop. In his frenzy, he lashes the crop at the man holding the fire hose. The man, resentfully, throws the end of the hose at* VACARRO, *who seizes the nozzle and walks directly towards and into the flames. Now men try to stop him.* VACARRO *turns the hose on them, driving them back and then goes into the flames. He disappears from sight. All we hear is his shouts in a foreign tongue.*

A wall collapses.

The hose suddenly leaps about as if it has been freed. The crowd. Horrified. Then they see something. . . . VACARRO *comes out. He holds aloft a small, gallon-size kerosene can. He strikes at his trouser bottoms, which are hot. He is on the point of collapse.*

Men rush to him and drag him to a safe distance. He clutches the can.

They lay him out, and crouch around him. He is smudged and singed. His eyes open, look around.

His viewpoint. From this distorted angle, lit by the victorious flames are a circle of faces which are either indifferent or down-right unfriendly. Some cannot control a faint smile.

VACARRO *clutches the can, closes his eyes.*

Another wall collapses.]

DISSOLVE.

31]

EXTERIOR. ARCHIE LEE'S HOUSE. NIGHT.

[ARCHIE LEE'S *car turns into the drive. He descends noiselessly as a thief. Camera follows him, and it and he discover* BABY DOLL *on the porch swing. There are several suitcases, packed and ready to go. In a chair near the porch swing, sleeping as mildly as a baby, is* AUNT ROSE COMFORT]

ARCHIE: What are you doin' out here at one o'clock in the morning?

BABY DOLL: I'm not talking to you.

ARCHIE: What are you doing out here?

BABY DOLL: Because in the first place, I didn't have the money to pay for a hotel room, because you don't give me any money, because you don't have any money, and secondly, because if I had the money I couldn't have no way of getting there because you went off in the Chevy, and leave me no way of getting anywhere, including to the fire which I wanted to see just like everyone else.

ARCHIE: What fire you talking about?

BABY DOLL: What fire am I talking about?

ARCHIE: I don't know about no fire.

BABY DOLL: You must be crazy or think I'm crazy. You mean to tell me you don't know the cotton gin burned down at the Syndicate Plantation right after you left the house.

ARCHIE: [*Seizing her arm*] Hush up. I never left this house.

28

BABY DOLL: You certainly did leave this house. ow!!

ARCHIE: Look here! Listen to what I tell you. I never left this house. . . .

BABY DOLL: You certainly did and left me here without a coke in the place. oww!! Cut it out!!

ARCHIE: Listen to what I tell you. I went up to bed with my bottle after supper –

BABY DOLL: What bed! ow!

ARCHIE: And passed out dead to the world. You got that in your haid?? Will you remember that now?

BABY DOLL: Let go my arm!

ARCHIE: What did I do after supper?

BABY DOLL: You know what you did, you jumped in the Chevy an' disappeared after supper and didn't get back till just – owww!!! Will you quit twisting my arm.

ARCHIE: I'm trying to wake you up. You're asleep, you're dreaming! What did I do after supper?

BABY DOLL: Went to bed! Leggo! Went to bed. Leggo! Leggo!

ARCHIE: That's right. Make sure you remember. I went to bed after supper and didn't wake up until I heard the fire whistle blow and I was too drunk to git up and drive the car. Now come inside and go to bed.

BABY DOLL: Go to what bed? I got no bed to go to!

ARCHIE: You will tomorrow. The furniture is coming back tomorrow.

[BABY DOLL *whimpers*.]

ARCHIE: [*Continues*] Did I hurt my little baby's arm?

BABY DOLL: Yais.

ARCHIE: Where I hurt little baby's arm?

BABY DOLL: Here. . . .

ARCHIE: [*He puts a big wet kiss on her arm*] Feel better?

BABY DOLL: No. . . .

ARCHIE: [*Another kiss. This travels up her arm*] My sweet baby doll. My sweet little baby doll.

BABY DOLL: [*Sleepily*] Hurt. . . . MMMmmmmm! Hurt.

ARCHIE: Hurt?

BABY DOLL: Mmm!

ARCHIE: Kiss?

BABY DOLL: Mmmmmmmmm!

ARCHIE: Baby sleepy?

BABY DOLL: MMmmmmm!

ARCHIE: Kiss good....?

BABY DOLL: Mmmmm....

ARCHIE: Make little room.... good....

BABY DOLL: Too hot.

ARCHIE: Make a little room, go on....

BABY DOLL: Mmmm....

ARCHIE: Whose baby? Big sweet.... whose baby?

BABY DOLL: You hurt me.... Mmmm....

ARCHIE: Kiss....

[*He lifts her wrist to his lips and makes gobbling sound. We get an idea of what their courtship – such as it was – was like. Also how passionately he craves her, willing to take her under any conditions, including fast asleep.*]

BABY DOLL: Stop it..., Silly.... Mmmmmm....

ARCHIE: What would I do if you was a big piece of cake?

BABY DOLL: Silly.

ARCHIE: Gobble! Gobble!

BABY DOLL: Oh you....

ARCHIE: What would I do if you was angel food cake? Big white piece with lots of nice thick icin'?

BABY DOLL: [*Giggling now, in spite of herself. She's also sleepy*] Quit.

ARCHIE: [*As close as he's ever been to having her*] Gobble! Gobble! Gobble!

BABY DOLL: Archie!

ARCHIE: Hmmmmm.... [*He's working on her arm*] Skrunch, gibble, ghrumpt ... etc.

BABY DOLL: You tickle....

ARCHIE: Answer little question....

BABY DOLL: What?

ARCHIE: [*Into her arm*] Where I been since supper?

BABY DOLL: Off in the Chevy –

[*Instantly he seizes her wrist again. She shrieks. The romance is over.*]

ARCHIE: Where I been since supper?

BABY DOLL: Upstairs....

ARCHIE: Doing what?

BABY DOLL: With your bottle. Archie, leggo....

ARCHIE: And what else....

BABY DOLL: Asleep. Leggo....

ARCHIE: [*Letting go*] Now you know where I been and what I been doing since supper. In case anybody asks.

BABY DOLL: Yeah.

ARCHIE: Now go to sleep....

[*He seizes her suitcases and goes off into the house.* BABY DOLL *follows, and* AUNT ROSE *follows her, asleep on her feet. As they go in,* ARCHIE LEE *comes out and looks around. Then he listens.*]

ARCHIE: Nice quiet night. Real nice and quiet.

[*The gin can no longer be heard.*]

CUT TO

32]

BRITE SPOT CAFE. EXTERIOR. NIGHT.

[*It's not quiet here at all. The area in front of the entrance is crowded with cars. A holiday mood prevails. It's as if the fire has satisfied some profound and basic hunger and left the people of that community exhilarated.*

The pick-up truck of SILVA VACARRO *drives up, shoots into a vacant spot. He leaps from the driver's cab. He has not yet washed, his shirt is torn and blackened and he has a crude bandage around the arm that holds the whip. He stands for a few moments beside his truck, looking around at the cars, trying to find the car of the* MARSHAL, *which would indicate that that county official is inside. Then he sees what he's looking for. He walks over to the car which has the official seal on its side, and not finding the* MARSHAL *there, turns and strides into the ...*]

33]

INTERIOR. BRITE SPOT. (A JUKE JOINT)

[*Everybody is talking about the fire. The juke box is a loud one. There are some dancing couples.*

SILVA VACARRO *passes by a little knot of men. He is followed by* ROCK, *holding the kerosene can. The camera stays with them. They smile.*]

A MAN: That ole boy is really burning!

[*One of the men detaches himself and moves in the direction that* VACARRO *took. Then another follows.*]

34]

GROUP OF MEN AROUND THE MARSHAL.

MARSHAL: What makes you think your gin was set fire to?

SILVA: Look around you. Did you ever see such a crowd of happy faces, looks like a rich man's funeral with all his relations attending.

MARSHAL: I'd hate to have to prove it.

SILVA: I'd hate to have to depend on you to prove it.

[*The man from the other group walks up.*]

MAN: What are you going to do about ginning out your cotton?

SILVA: I'll truck it over to Sunset. Collins'll gin it out for me.

MAN: Collins got cotton of his own to gin.

SILVA: Then I'll truck it across the river. Ain't nobody around here's gonna gin it.

MAN: I'm all set up to do it for you.

SILVA: I wouldn't give you the satisfaction.

[*The men drift back a few steps.*]

MARSHAL: [*He speaks a little for the benefit of the men in the room*] I honestly can't imagine if it was a case of arson who could of done it since every man jack that you put out of business was standing right there next to the platform when the fire broke out.

ROCK: One wasn't. I know one that wasn't.

MARSHAL: [*Wheeling on bar-stool to face him. Sharply*] Looky here, boy! Naming names is risky, just on suspicion.

ROCK: I didn't name his name. I just said I know it. And the initials are stamped on this here can.

MARSHAL: [*Quickly*] Let's break it up, break it up, not the time or the place to make accusations, I'll take charge of this can. I'll examine it carefully to see if there's any basis for thinking it was used to start a fire with.

SILVA: [*Cutting in*] I run through fire to git that can, and I mean to keep it. [*Then to* ROCK]
Lock it up in the pick-up truck.

[ROCK *leaves. Unobtrusively some men follow him.*]

MARSHAL: Vacarro. Come over here. I want to have a word with you in one of these booths. . . .

35]

ROCK.

[*He enters the men's room. As he approaches the urinal, the light is switched out and the door is thrown open at the same moment. Hoarse muffled shouts and sounds of struggle and a metallic clatter. Then the light goes on and* ROCK *is lying on the filthy cement floor, dazed.* VACARRO *enters. He goes to* ROCK.]

ROCK: They got the can, boss.

SILVA: Whose initials was on it? Huh? You said you seen some initials on the can.

ROCK: Naw. It just said – Sears and Roebuck.

[*The* MARSHAL *has come in and now reaches down and helps* ROCK *to regain his feet. . . .*]

MARSHAL: Sears and Roebuck! That does it! Hahaha. Boy, git up and git some black coffee in yuh.

[*They pass through the door.*]

36]

THE MAIN ROOM.

MARSHAL: Ruby, Ruby! Give this boy some black coffee. He had a bad fall in the outhouse. Hawhawhaw. . . .

[*But* SILVA *has steered* ROCK *out the front door and they are gone. The* MARSHAL *follows* . . .]

37]

OUTSIDE.

[SILVA *and* ROCK *head towards the pick-up. The* MARSHAL appears in the doorway.]

MARSHAL: Vacarro!

[SILVA *and* ROCK *are at the truck. They wait for the* MARSHAL, *who is walking towards them.*]

MARSHAL: [*Soberly, plainly*] You take the advice of an old man who knows this county like the back of his hand. It's true you made a lot of enemies here. You happen to be a man with foreign blood. That's a disadvantage in this county. A disadvantage at least to begin with. But you added stubbornness and suspicion and resentment.

[VACARRO *makes an indescribable sound.*]

MARSHAL: I still say, a warm, friendly attitude on your part could have overcome that quickly. Instead, you stood off from people, refused to fraternize with them. Why not drop that attitude now? If someone set fire to your gin – I say that's not impossible. Also, I say we'll find him. But I don't have to tell you that if you now take your cotton across the river, or into another county, it will give rise to a lot of unfriendly speculation. No one would like it. No one.

[*Abruptly he turns and goes.*

ROCK *and* SILVA *are left alone. Men watch them from the surrounding cars . . . from the doorway.*]

SILVA: Did you ever see so many happy faces? Which one did it, Rock, you said you knew . . .?

ROCK: Well, they're all here . . . all here except one. The one that ain't here, I figure he did it. . . .

[*They're getting into the pick-up.*]

SILVA: Well, he's the one that's gonna gin out my cotton . . . .

[*The motor starts . . . the car goes into gear . . . and moves.*]

DISSOLVE.

38]

THE ROAD BEFORE ARCHIE LEE'S HOUSE. THE NEXT MORNING.

[SILVA'S *pick-up truck is leading a long line of cotton wagons — full of cotton.*]

39]

CLOSER SHOT. THE PICK-UP.
[*It stops.*]

40]

CLOSE ANGLE. SILVA AND ROCK.

ROCK: Maybe it figures. But it sure puzzles me why you want to bring your cotton to the guy that burned down your gin. . . .

SILVA: You don't know the Christian proverbs about how you turn the other cheek when one has been slapped. . . .

ROCK: When both cheeks has been kicked, what are you gonna turn then?

SILVA: You just got to turn and keep turning. Stop the wagons! I'm gonna drive up to his house.

[ROCK *bops out of the pick-up truck.*]

41]

OUTSIDE MEIGHAN HOUSE.
[*At an upstairs window we can just see* ARCHIE'S *face. He is watching the wagons. Suddenly, he withdraws his head.*]

42]

UPSTAIRS. ARCHIE LEE MEIGHAN'S HOUSE.
[*He goes into a crazy, but silent Indian war dance. Then suddenly he can no longer contain himself and runs into* . . .

43]

THE NURSERY
[*Enter* ARCHIE LEE.

BABY DOLL *is asleep in the crib. Her thumb is in her mouth.*
Like a child, she's trying to hold on to her sleep.
ARCHIE LEE *just whoops and hollers.* 'Baby Doll! Baby
Doll!', *etc.* 'Get up . . .' *etc.*
She can hardly believe her eyes. . . .
From downstairs the pick-up's horn sounds urgently.
AUNT ROSE COMFORT *rushes in breathlessly . . .*]

AUNT ROSE: Archie Lee, honesy. . . .

ARCHIE: [*Very Big Shot*] Get her up! Get her up, get her
washed and dressed and looking decent. Then bring her
down. The furniture is coming back today. . . .

[*He exits. . . .*]

44/65]

FRONT YARD.

[SILVA *and* ROCK *are sitting there in the pick-up truck. They
sit a little formally and stiffly and wait for* MEIGHAN, *who
comes barrelling out of the house, and up to the pick-up.*]

ARCHIE: Don't say a word. A little bird already told me that
you'd be bringing those twenty-seven wagons full of cotton
straight to my door, and I want you to know that you're a
very lucky fellow.

ROCK: [*Dryly*] How come?

ARCHIE: I mean that I am in a position to hold back other
orders and give you a priority. Well! Come on out of that
truck and have some coffee.

SILVA: What's your price?

ARCHIE: You remember my price. It hasn't changed.

[*Silence. The sense that* SILVA *is inspecting him.*]

ARCHIE: Hey, now looka here. Like you take shirts to a
laundry. You take them Friday and you want them Saturday. That's special. You got to pay special.

SILVA: How about your equipment? Hasn't changed either?

ARCHIE: A-1 shape! Always was! You ought to remember.

SILVA: I remember you needed a new saw-cylinder. You got
one?

ARCHIE: Can't find one on the market to equal the old one yet. Come on down and have a cup of coffee. We're all ready for you.

SILVA: I guess when you saw my gin burning down last night you must've suspected that you might get a good deal of business thrown your way in the morning.

ARCHIE: You want to know something?

SILVA: I'm always glad to know something when there's something to know.

[ROCK *laughs wildly*.]

ARCHIE: I never seen that fire of yours last night! Now come on over to my house and have some coffee.

[*The men get out of the truck.* ARCHIE *speaks to* ROCK.]

ARCHIE: You come too, if you want to. . . . No, sir, I never seen that fire of yours last night. We hit the sack right after supper and didn't know until breakfast time this morning that your cotton gin had burned down.

[*They go up on the porch.*]

Yes sir, it's providential. That's the only word for it. Hey, Baby Doll! It's downright providential. Baby Doll! Come out here, Baby Doll!

[*Enter* BABY DOLL.]

You come right over here and meet Mr Vacarro from the Syndicate Plantation.

BABY DOLL: Oh hello. Has something gone wrong, Archie Lee?

ARCHIE: What do you mean, Baby Doll?

BABY DOLL: I just thought that maybe something went –

ARCHIE: What is your first name, Vacarro?

SILVA: Silva.

ARCHIE: How do you spell it?

[SILVA *spells it.* '*Capital S-I-L-V-A.*' *Meantime, his eyes on* BABY DOLL.]

ARCHIE: Oh. Like a silver lining? Every cloud has got a silver lining.

BABY DOLL: What is that from? The Bible?

SILVA: No, the Mother Goose book.

BABY DOLL: That name sounds foreign.

SILVA: It is, Mrs Meighan. I'm known as the wop that runs the Syndicate Plantation.

[ARCHIE LEE *claps him heartily on the back.* SILVA *stiffly withdraws from the contact.*]

ARCHIE: Don't call yourself names. Let other folks call you names! Well, you're a lucky little fellow, silver, gold, or even nickel-plated, you sure are lucky that I can take a job of this size right now. It means some cancellations, but you're my closest neighbour. I believe in the good-neighbour policy, Mr Vacarro. You do me a good turn and I'll do you a good turn. Tit for tat. Tat for tit is the policy we live on. *Aunt Rose Comfort!* Baby Doll, git your daddy's ole maid sister to break out a fresh pot of coffee for Mr Vacarro.

BABY DOLL: You get her.

ARCHIE: And honey, I want you to entertain this gentleman. Ha! Ha! Look at her blush. Haha! This is my baby. This is my little girl, every precious ounce of her is mine, all mine.

[*He exits – crazily elated, calling 'Aunt Rose'.*

CUT BACK to BABY DOLL. *She emits an enormous yawn.*]

BABY DOLL: Excuse my yawn. We went to bed kinda late last night.

CUT TO SILVA. He notices the discrepancy. He looks at ROCK, *who also noticed.*

As if she were talking of a title of great distinction.]

So. You're a wop?

SILVA: [*With ironic politeness*] I'm a Sicilian, Mrs Meighan. A very ancient people. . . .

BABY DOLL: [*Trying out the word*] Sish! Sish!

SILVA: No, ma'am. Siss! Sicilian.

BABY DOLL: Oh, how unusual.

[ARCHIE LEE *bursts back out on the porch.*]

ARCHIE: And honey, at noon, take Mr Vacarro in town to the Kotton King Hotel for a chicken dinner. Sign my name! It's only when bad luck hits you, Mr Vacarro, that you find out who your friends are. I mean to prove it. All right. Let's get GOING! Baby, knock me a kiss!

BABY DOLL: What's the matter with you? Have you got drunk before breakfast?

ARCHIE: Hahaha.

BABY DOLL: Somebody say something funny?

ARCHIE: Offer this young fellow here to a cup of coffee. I got to get busy ginning that cotton. [*He extends his great sweaty hand to* VACARRO.] Glad to be able to help you out of this bad situation. It's the good-neighbour policy.

SILVA: What is?

ARCHIE: You do me a good turn and I'll do you a good turn some time in the future.

SILVA: I see.

ARCHIE: Tit for tat, tat for tit, as they say. Hahaha! Well, make yourself at home here. Baby Doll, I want you to make this gentleman comfortable in the house.

BABY DOLL: You can't make anyone comfortable in this house. Lucky if you can find a chair to sit in.

[*But* MEIGHAN *is gone, calling out, 'Move those wagons', etc., etc.*]

BABY DOLL: [*After a slight pause*] Want some coffee?

SILVA: No. Just a cool drink of water, thank you, ma'am.

BABY DOLL: The kitchen water runs warm, but if you got the energy to handle an old-fashioned pump, you can get you a real cool drink from that there cistern at the side of the house. . . .

SILVA: I got energy to burn.

[VACARRO *strides through the tall seeding grass to an old cistern with a hand pump, deep in the side yard.* ROCK *follows.* OLD FUSSY *goes 'Squawk, Squawk', and* AUNT ROSE COMFORT *is singing 'Rock of Ages' in the kitchen.*]

SILVA: [*Looking about contemptuously as he crosses to the cistern*] Dump their garbage in the yard, phew! *Ignorance* and *Indulgence* and *stink*!

ROCK: I thought that young Mizz Meighan smelt pretty good.

SILVA: You keep your nose with the cotton. And hold that dipper, I'll pump.

AUNT ROSE: Sometimes water comes and sometimes it don't.

[*The water comes pouring from the rusty spout.*]

SILVA: This time it did. . . .

BABY DOLL: Bring me a dipper of that nice cool well water, please.

[ROCK *crosses immediately with the filled dipper.*]

SILVA: Hey!

OLD FUSSY: Squawk, squawk!!

AUNT ROSE: I don't have the strength any more in my arm that I used to, to draw water out of that pump.

[*She approaches, smoothing her ancient apron.* VACARRO *is touched by her aged grace.*]

SILVA: Would you care for a drink?

AUNT ROSE: How do you do? I'm Aunt Rose Comfort McCorkle. My brother was Baby Doll's daddy, Mr T. C. Carson. I've been visiting here since . . . since . . . [*She knits her ancient brow, unable to recall precisely when the long visit started.*]

SILVA: I hope you don't mind drinking out of a gourd.

[*He hands her the gourd of well water.* ROCK *returns, saying aloud* . . .

ROCK: I could think of worse ways to spend a hot afternoon than delivering cool well water to Mrs Meighan.

AUNT ROSE: SCUSE ME PLEASE! That ole hen, Fussy, has just gone back in my kitchen!

[*She runs crazily to the house.* BABY DOLL *has wandered back to the cistern as if unconsciously drawn by the magnetism of the two young males.*]

BABY DOLL: They's such a difference in water! You wouldn't think so, but there certainly is.

SILVA: [*To* ROCK] Hold the dipper, I'll pump!

[*He brings up more water; then strips off his shirt and empties the brimming dipper over his head and at the same time he says to* ROCK . . .]

SILVA: Go stay with the cotton. Go on! Stay with the cotton.

[ROCK *goes.*]

BABY DOLL: I wouldn't dare to expose myself like that. I take such terrible sunburn.

SILVA: I like the feel of a hot sun on my body.

BABY DOLL: That's not sunburn though. You're natcherally dark.

SILVA: Yes. Don't you have garbage collectors on Tiger Tail Road?

BABY DOLL: It cost a little bit extra to git them to come out here and Archie Lee Meighan claimed it was highway robbery! Refused to pay! Now the place is swarming with flies an' mosquitoes and – oh, I don't know, I almost give up sometimes.

SILVA: And did I understand you to say that you've got a bunch of unfurnished rooms in the house?

BABY DOLL: Five complete sets of furniture hauled away! By the Ideal Pay As You Go Plan Furniture Company.

SILVA: When did this misfortune – fall upon you?

BABY DOLL: Why, yestiddy! Ain't that awful?

SILVA: Both of us had misfortunes on the same day.

BABY DOLL: Huh?

SILVA: You lost your furniture. My cotton gin burned down.

BABY DOLL: [Not quite with it] Oh.

SILVA: Quite a coincidence!

BABY DOLL: Huh?

SILVA: I said it was a coincidence of misfortune.

BABY DOLL: Well, sure – after all what can you do with a bunch of unfurnished rooms.

SILVA: Well, you could play hide-and-seek.

BABY DOLL: Not me. I'm not athletic.

SILVA: I take it you've not had this place long, Mrs Meighan.

BABY DOLL: No, we ain't had it long.

SILVA: When I arrived in this county to take over the management of the Syndicate Plantation ... [Chops at grass with crop] this place was empty. I was told it was haunted. Then you all moved in.

BABY DOLL: Yes it was haunted, and that's why Archie Lee bought it for almost nothing. [She pauses in the sun as if dazed] Sometimes I don't know where to go, what to do.

SILVA: That's not uncommon. People enter this world without instruction.

BABY DOLL: [She's lost him again] Huh?

SILVA: I said people come into this world without instructions of where to go, what to do, so they wander a little and ...

[AUNT ROSE *sings rather sweetly from the kitchen, wind blows an Aeolian refrain.*]

then go away....

[*Now* BABY DOLL *gives him a quick look, almost perceptive and then* ...]

BABY DOLL: Yah, well ...

SILVA: *Drift* – for a while and then ... *vanish.* [*He stoops to pick a dandelion*] And so make room for newcomers! Old goers, newcomers! Back and forth, going and coming, rush, rush!! *Permanent? Nothing!* [*Blows on the seeding dandelion*] Anything living! ... last long enough to take it serious.

[*They are walking together. There is the beginning of some weird understanding between them.*

They have stopped strolling by a poetic wheelless chassis of an old Pierce-Arrow limousine in the side yard.]

BABY DOLL: This is the old Pierce-Arrow car that belonged to the lady that used to own this place and haunts it now.

[VACARRO *steps gravely forward and opens the back door for her.*]

SILVA: Where to, madam?

BABY DOLL: Oh, you're playing *show-fer!* It's a good place to sit when the house isn't furnished....

[*She enters and sinks on the ruptured upholstery. He gravely puts the remnant of the dandelion in the cone-shaped cut-glass vase in a bracket by the back seat of the old limousine.*]

BABY DOLL: [*Laughing with sudden, childish laughter*] Drive me along the river as fast as you can with all the windows open to cool me off.

SILVA: Fine, madam!

BABY DOLL: [*Suddenly aware of his body near her*] Showfers sit in the front seat.

SILVA: Front seat's got no cushion.

BABY DOLL: It's hard to find a place to sit around here since

the Ideal Pay As You Go Plan people lost patience. To sit
in comfort, I mean. . . .

SILVA: It's hard to sit in comfort when the Ideal Pay As You Go
Plan people lose their patience and your gin burns down.

BABY DOLL: Oh! But . . .

SILVA: Huh?

BABY DOLL: You said that like you thought there was . . .

SILVA: What?

BABY DOLL: Some connexion! Excuse me, I want to get out
and I can't get over your legs. . . .

[*Her apathy is visited by a sudden inexplicable flurry of panic.
He has his boots propped against the back of the front seat.*]

SILVA: You can't get over my legs?

BABY DOLL: No. I'm not athletic.

[*She tries to open door on other side, but it is blocked by the
trunk of a pecan tree.*]

SILVA: But it's cool here and comfortable to sit in. What's
this here??

[*He has seized her wrist on which hangs a bracelet of many little
gold charms. She sinks somewhat uneasily in beside him.*]

BABY DOLL: It's a, it's a . . . charm bracelet.

[*He begins to finger the many little gold charms attached.*]

BABY DOLL: My daddy gave it to me. Them there's the ten
commandments.

SILVA: And these?

BABY DOLL: My birthdays. It's stretchable. One for each
birthday.

SILVA: How many charming birthdays have you had?

BABY DOLL: As many as I got charms hanging on that
bracelet.

SILVA: Mind if I count 'em? [*They are close.*] Fourteen, fifteen,
sixteen, seventeen, eighteen, nineteen, and . . .

BABY DOLL: That's all. I'll be twenty tomorrow. Tomorrow
is Election Day and Election Day is my birthday. I was
born on the day that Frank Delano Roosevelt was elected
for his first term.

SILVA: A great day for the country for both reasons.

BABY DOLL: He was a man to respect.

SILVA: And you're a lady to respect, Mrs Meighan.

BABY DOLL: [*Sadly and rather touchingly*] Me? Oh, no – I never got past the fourth grade.

SILVA: Why'd you quit?

BABY DOLL: I had a great deal of trouble with long division.
. . .

SILVA: Yeah?

BABY DOLL: The teacher would tell me to go to the blackboard and work out a problem in long division and I would go to the blackboard and lean my head against it and cry and cry and – cry. . . .
Whew! I think the porch would be cooler. Mr Vacarro, I can't get over your legs.

SILVA: You want to move my legs.

BABY DOLL: Yes, otherwise I can't get out of the car. . . .

SILVA: Okay.
[*He raises his legs so she can get out. Which she does, and continues . . .*]

BABY DOLL: YES, I would cry and cry. . . . Well . . . soon after that I left school. A girl without education is – without education. . . . Whew. . . . Feel kind of dizzy. Hope I'm not gettin' a *sun* stroke. – I better sit in the shade. . . .
[VACARRO *follows her casually into the shade of the pecan tree where there's a decrepit old swing. Suddenly, he leaps into branches and then down with a pecan. He cracks it in his mouth and hands her the kernels. . . .*]

BABY DOLL: Mr Vacarro! I wouldn't dream! – excuse me, but I just wouldn't dream! of eating a nut that a man had cracked in his mouth. . . .

SILVA: You've got many refinements. I don't think you need to worry about your failure at long division. I mean, after all, you got through short division, and short division is all that a lady ought to be called on to cope with. . . .

BABY DOLL: Well, I – ought to go in, but I get depressed when I pass through those empty rooms. . . .

SILVA: All the rooms empty?

BABY DOLL: All but the nursery. And the kitchen. The stuff in those rooms was paid for. . .

SILVA: You have a child in the nursery?

BABY DOLL: Me? No. I sleep in the nursery myself. Let down the slats on the crib. . . .

SILVA: Why do you sleep in the nursery?

BABY DOLL: Mr Vacarro, that's a *personal* question.
[*There is a pause.*]

BABY DOLL: I ought to go in . . . but . . . you know there are places in that house which I never been in. I mean the attic for instance. Most of the time I'm afraid to go into that house by myself. Last night when the fire broke out I sat here on this swing for hours and hours till Archie Lee got home, because I was scared to enter this old place by myself.
[*VACARRO has caught this discrepancy too.*]

SILVA: It musta been scary here without your husband to look after you.

BABY DOLL: I'm tellin' you! The fire lit up the whole country-side and it made big crazy shadows and we didn't have a coke in the house and the heat and the mosquitoes and – I was mad at Archie Lee.

SILVA: Mad at Mr Meighan? What about?

BABY DOLL: Oh, he went off and left me settin' here without a coke in the place.

SILVA: Went off and left you, did he??!!

BABY DOLL: Well, he certainly did. Right after supper and when he got back, the fire'd already broke out. I got smoke in my eyes and my nose and throat. I was in such a worn-out nervous condition it made me cry. Finally I took two teaspoons of paregoric.

SILVA: Sounds like you passed a very uncomfortable night.

BABY DOLL: Sounds like? Well it was!

SILVA: So Mr Meighan – you say – disappeared after supper.

BABY DOLL: [*After a pause*] Huh?

SILVA: You say Mr Meighan left the house for a while after supper?
[*Something in his tone makes her aware that she has spoken indiscreetly.*]

BABY DOLL: Oh – uh – just for a moment.

SILVA: Just for a moment, huh? How long a moment?

BABY DOLL: What are you driving at, Mr Vacarro?

SILVA: Driving at? Nothing.

BABY DOLL: You're looking at me so funny.

SILVA: How long a moment did he disappear for? Can you remember, Mrs Meighan?

BABY DOLL: What difference does that make? What's it to you, anyhow?

SILVA: Why should you mind my asking?

BABY DOLL: You make this sound like I was on trial for something.

SILVA: Don't you like to pretend like you're a witness?

BABY DOLL: Witness of what, Mr Vacarro?

SILVA: Why – for instance – say – a case of arson!

BABY DOLL: Case of –? What is – arson?

SILVA: The wilful destruction of property by fire. [*Slaps his boots sharply with the riding crop*]

BABY DOLL: Oh! [*She nervously fingers her purse*]

SILVA: There's one thing I always notice about you ladies.

BABY DOLL: What's that?

SILVA: Whenever you get nervous, you always like to have something in your hands to hold on to – like that big white purse.

BABY DOLL: This purse?

SILVA: Yes, it gives you something to hold on to, isn't that right?

BABY DOLL: Well, I do always like to have something in my hands.

SILVA: Sure you do. You feel what a lot of uncertain things there are. Gins burn down. No one know how or why. Volunteer fire departments don't have decent equipment. They're no protection. The afternoon sun is too hot. The trees! They're no protection! The house – it's haunted! It's no protection. Your husband. He's across the road and busy. He's no protection! The goods that dress is made of – it's light and thin – it's no protection. So what do you do, Mrs Meighan? You pick up that white kid purse. It's something to hold on to.

46

BABY DOLL: Now, Mr Silva. Don't you go and be getting any – funny ideas.

SILVA: Ideas about what?

BABY DOLL: My husband disappearing – after supper. I can explain that.

SILVA: Can you?

BABY DOLL: Sure I can.

SILVA: Good! How do you explain it? [*He stares at her. She looks down*] What's the matter? Can't you collect your thoughts, Mrs Meighan?

[*Pause*]

Your mind's a blank on the subject??

BABY DOLL: Look here, now. . . .

SILVA: You find it impossible to remember just what your husband disappeared for after supper? You can't imagine what kind of an errand he went out on, can you?

BABY DOLL: No! No! I can't!

SILVA: But when he returned – let's see – the fire had just broken out at the Syndicate Plantation.

BABY DOLL: Mr Vacarro, I don't have the slightest idea what you could be driving at.

SILVA: You're a very unsatisfactory witness, Mrs Meighan.

BABY DOLL: I never can think when people – stare straight at me.

SILVA: Okay, I'll look away then. [*Turns his back to her*] Now, does that improve your memory any? Now are you able to concentrate on the question?

BABY DOLL: Huh?

SILVA: No? You're not? [*Grins evilly*] Well – should we drop the subject??

BABY DOLL: Sure do wish you would!

SILVA: Sure, there's no use crying over a burnt-down gin. And besides, like your husband says – this world is built on the principle of tit for tat.

BABY DOLL: What do you mean?

SILVA: Nothing at all specific. Mind if I . . .?

BABY DOLL: What?

[SILVA *approaches the swing where she sits.*]

47

SILVA: You want to move over a little and make some room?

BABY DOLL: [*Shifts slightly*] Is that room enough for you?

SILVA: Enough for me. How about you?

BABY DOLL: Is it strong enough to support us both?

SILVA: I hope. Let's swing a little. You seem all tense. Motion relaxes people. It's like a cradle. A cradle relaxes a baby. They call you 'Baby', don't they?

BABY DOLL: That's sort of a pet name.

SILVA: Well in the swing you can relax like a cradle. . . .

BABY DOLL: Not if you swing it so high. It shakes me up.

SILVA: Well, I'll swing it low then. Are you relaxed?

BABY DOLL: I'm relaxed enough. As much as necessary.

SILVA: No, you're not. Your nerves are tied up.

BABY DOLL: You make me nervous.

SILVA: Just swinging with you?

BABY DOLL: Not just that.

SILVA: What else then?

BABY DOLL: All them questions you asked me about the fire.

SILVA: I only inquired about your husband – about his leaving the house after supper.

BABY DOLL: Why should I have to explain why he left the house? Besides, I did. I think I explained that to you.

SILVA: You said that he left the house before the fire broke out.

BABY DOLL: What about it?

SILVA: Why did he leave the house?

BABY DOLL: I explained that to you. I explained that to you.

SILVA: What was the explanation? I forgot it.

[BABY DOLL'*s face is beaded with sweat. To save her life she can't think, can't think at all.*]

BABY DOLL: [*Just to gain a moment*] Oh, you're talking about my husband?

SILVA: That's who I'm talking about.

BABY DOLL: How should I know!!!

SILVA: You mean where he went after supper.

BABY DOLL: Yes!! How should I know where he went.

SILVA: I thought you said you explained that to me.

BABY DOLL: I did! I explained it to you!

SILVA: Well, if you don't know, how could you explain it to me?

BABY DOLL: [*Turning*] There's no reason why I should explain things to you.

SILVA: Then just relax.

[*They swing.*]

As I was saying, that was a lovely remark your husband made.

BABY DOLL: What remark did he make?

SILVA: The good-neighbour policy. I see what he means by that now.

BABY DOLL: He was talking about the President's speech.

SILVA: I think he was talking about something closer to home. *You do me* a good turn and *I'll do you* one. That was the way he put it. [*Delicately he removes a little piece of lint from her arm.*]

SILVA: There now!

BABY DOLL: [*Nervously*] Thanks.

SILVA: There's a lot of fine cotton lint floating around in the air.

BABY DOLL: I know there is. It irritates my sinus.

SILVA: Well, you're a delicate woman.

BABY DOLL: Delicate? Me? Oh no. I'm a good-size woman.

SILVA: There's a lot of you, but every bit of you is delicate. Choice. Delectable, I might say.

BABY DOLL: Huh?

SILVA: [*Running his finger lightly over her skin*] You're fine fibred. And smooth. And soft.

BABY DOLL: Our conversation is certainly taking a personal turn!

SILVA: Yes! You make me think of cotton. [*Still caressing her arm another moment*] No! No fabric, no kind of cloth, not even satin or silk cloth, or no kind of fibre, not even cotton fibre has the ab-so-lute delicacy of your skin!

BABY DOLL: Well! Should I say thanks or something?

SILVA: No, just smile, Mrs Meighan. You have an attractive smile. Dimples!!

BABY DOLL: No . . .

49

SILVA: Yes, you have! Smile, Mrs Meighan! Come on! Smile!
  [BABY DOLL *averts her face, smiles helplessly.*]
  There now. See? You've got them! [*Delicately, he touches one of the indentations in her cheek.*]

BABY DOLL: Please don't touch me. I don't like to be touched.

SILVA: Then why do you giggle?

BABY DOLL: Can't help it. You make me feel kind of hysterical, Mr Vacarro ... Mr Vacarro ...

SILVA: Yes?

BABY DOLL: [*A different attack, more feminine, pleading*] I hope you don't think that Archie Lee was mixed up in that fire. I swear to goodness he never left the front porch. I remember it perfectly now. We just set here on the swing till the fire broke out and then we drove into town.

SILVA: To celebrate!

BABY DOLL: No, no, no!

SILVA: Twenty-seven wagons full of cotton's a pretty big piece of business to fall into your lap like a gift from the gods, Mrs Meighan.

BABY DOLL: I thought you said we would drop the subject.

SILVA: You brought it up that time.

BABY DOLL: Well, please don't try to mix me up any more, I swear to goodness the fire had already broke out when he got back.

SILVA: That's not what you told me a moment ago.

BABY DOLL: You got me all twisted up. We went in town. The fire broke out and we didn't know about it.

SILVA: I thought you said it irritated your sinus.

BABY DOLL: Oh my God, you sure put words in my mouth. Maybe I'd better make us some lemonade.
  [*She starts to get up. Silva pulls her down.*]
  What did you do that for?

SILVA: I don't want to be deprived of your company yet. [*He lightly switches her legs with his crop.*]

BABY DOLL: [*Twisting*] Mr Vacarro, you're getting awfully familiar.

SILVA: Haven't you got any fun-loving spirit about you?

BABY DOLL: This isn't fun.

SILVA: Then why do you giggle?

BABY DOLL: I'm ticklish!

SILVA: Ticklish!

BABY DOLL: Yes, quit switching me, will you?

SILVA: I'm just shooing the flies off.

BABY DOLL: They don't hurt nothing. And would you mind moving your arm?

SILVA: Don't be so skittish!

BABY DOLL: All right! I'll get up then.

SILVA: Go on.

BABY DOLL: [*Trying*] I feel so weak. [*She pulls herself away from him*] Oh! My head's so buzzy.

SILVA: Fuzzy?

BABY DOLL: Fuzzy and buzzy. My head's swinging around. It's that swinging.... Is something on my arm?

SILVA: No.

BABY DOLL: Then what are you brushing?

SILVA: Sweat off. Let me wipe it.... [*He brushes her arm with his handkerchief.*]

BABY DOLL: [*Laughing weakly*] No, please don't. It feels funny.

SILVA: How does it feel?

BABY DOLL: Funny! All up and down. You cut it out now. If you don't cut it out I'm going to call.

SILVA: Call who?

BABY DOLL: That nigger who's cuttin' the grass across the road.

SILVA: Go on. Call then.

BABY DOLL: Hey! [*Her voice is faint, weak*] Hey, boy, boy!

SILVA: Can't you call any louder?

BABY DOLL: I feel so funny! What's the matter with me?

SILVA: You're just relaxing. You're big. There's a lot of you and it's all relaxing. So give in. Stop getting yourself all excited.

BABY DOLL: I'm not – but you....

SILVA: I!???

BABY DOLL: Yes. You. Suspicions. The ideas you have about my husband ... suspicions.

SILVA: Suspicions? Such as ...

BABY DOLL: Such as he burnt your gin down.

SILVA: Well?

BABY DOLL: He didn't.

SILVA: Didn't he?

BABY DOLL: I'm going inside. I'm going in the house.
  [*She starts in. He follows close beside her.*]

SILVA: But you're afraid of the house! Do you believe in ghosts, Mrs Meighan? I do. I believe in the presence of evil spirits.

BABY DOLL: What evil spirits you talking about now?

SILVA: Spirits of violence – and cunning – malevolence – cruelty – treachery – destruction....

BABY DOLL: Oh, them's just human characteristics.

SILVA: They're evil spirits that haunt the human heart and take possession of it, and spread from one human heart to another human heart the way that a fire goes springing from leaf to leaf and branch to branch in a tree till a forest is all aflame with it – the birds take flight – the wild things are suffocated ... everything green and beautiful is destroyed....

BABY DOLL: You have got fire on the brain.

SILVA: I see it as more than it seems to be on the surface. I saw it last night as an explosion of those evil spirits that haunt the human heart – I fought it! I ran into it, beating it, stamping it, shouting the curse of God at it! They dragged me out, suffocating. I was defeated! When I came to, lying on the ground – the fire had won the battle, and all around was a ring of human figures! The fire lit their faces! I looked up. And they were illuminated! Their eyes, their teeth were SHINING!! SEE! LIKE THIS! [*He twists his face into a grotesque grimace of pleasure. He holds her. They have arrived at the door to the interior of the house.*] Yeah! Like this! Like this!! [*He thrusts his grimacing face at her. She springs back, frightened.*]

BABY DOLL: Hey! Please! Don't do that! Don't scare me!

SILVA: The faces I saw – were grinning! Then I knew! I knew the fire was not accidental! [*He holds her fast at the door.*]

BABY DOLL: [*Weakly*] Not accidental?

SILVA: No, it was not accidental! It was an expression, a manifestation of the human will to *destroy*.

BABY DOLL: I wouldn't – feel that way – about it. . . .

SILVA: I do! I do! And so I say I believe in ghosts, in haunted places, places haunted by the people that occupy them with hearts overrun by demons of hate and destruction. I believe this place, this house is haunted. . . . What's the matter?

BABY DOLL: [*Now thoroughly shaken*] I don't know. . . .

SILVA: You're scared to enter the house, is that the trouble?

BABY DOLL: [*Calling*] Aunt Rose. Aunt Rose! ! [*No answer*] That old woman can't hear a thing.

SILVA: There's no question about it. This place is haunted.

BABY DOLL: I'm getting – I'm getting so thirsty, so hot and thirsty!

SILVA: Then why don't you treat yourself to a drink of cold water?

BABY DOLL: I – I thought I might make us a – pitcher of – cold lemonade.

[*For some reason,* BABY DOLL *doesn't want to enter the front door and she starts around the porch away from him. A board cracks under her weight. She screams, staggers.* SILVA *rushes to her and seizes her plump arm, placing an arm behind her. She giggles weakly, but for the first time accepting his help.*]

BABY DOLL: The place is – collapsing right underneath me!

SILVA: You're trembling, Mrs Meighan, shaking all over!

BABY DOLL: Your – your hands are so – hot – I don't think I ever felt hands as hot as your hands, they're – why they're like a couple of plates – took right out of – the oven!

SILVA: Burn, do they?

BABY DOLL: Yeah, they – *do*, they *burn* – me. . . .

SILVA: The idea of lemonade is very attractive. I would be glad to help you squeeze the lemons. [*Tightens the pressure of his hands.*]

BABY DOLL: I know you would! I mean I – thanks, but – I can do it myself.

SILVA: You don't want my assistance, Mrs Meighan?

BABY DOLL: Naw, it ain't necessary. . . .

SILVA: But then you would have to go into the house alone and the house is haunted! I better go in with you!

BABY DOLL: . . . No, it ain't necessary! [*She is panting.*]

SILVA: You want me to stay on the porch?

BABY DOLL: Yeh, you stay on the porch!

SILVA: Why *shouldn't* I come inside?

BABY DOLL: No reason, just – just . . . ! [*She giggles weakly*] You stay out here while I make the lemonade and . . .

SILVA: All right. Go on, Mrs Meighan. . . .

BABY DOLL: You stay out here. . . .

[*He doesn't answer. She stares at him, not moving.*]

SILVA: Now what's the matter now? Why don't you go in?

BABY DOLL: I don't think I better. I think I will go across the road to the gin. They got a water cooler. . . .

SILVA: The water cooler's for coloured. A lady, a white lady like you, the wife of the big white boss, would place herself in an undignified position if she went over the road to drink with the hands! They might get notions about her! Unwholesome ideas! The sight of her soft white flesh, so smooth and abundant, might inflame their – natures . . .

[*Suddenly* BABY DOLL *sees something off and . . .*]

66]

NEGRO BOY COMING DOWN THE ROAD.

[*He pushes a lawnmower. Behind him can be seen* ARCHIE LEE's *gin, working.*]

67]

BABY DOLL.

[*She rushes past* SILVA *in the direction of the Negro boy, runs unsteadily as if she were drunk, across the unkempt lawn and out into the shimmering brilliance of the road.*]

BABY DOLL: Boy! Boy! I want you to cut my grass.

BOY: Can't now, ma'am.

BABY DOLL: Yes, you can.

BOY: I got a job cuttin' grass across Tiger Tail Bayou.

BABY DOLL: You cut grass here. [*Her intensity frightens the boy.*]

BOY: Yes, ma'am, later.

BABY DOLL: NO! NOW! RIGHT NOW! I – I'll pay you five dollars. . . .

BOY: Yes, ma'am.

BABY DOLL: I'll pay you five dollars . . . but *now.*

BOY: [*Scared to death*] Yes, ma'am. Yes, ma'am.

BABY DOLL: And work close to the house. Hear! Speak up. Do you hear . . .?

BOY: Yes, ma'am. Yes, ma'am.

[BABY DOLL *sees* . . .]

68]

SILVA.

[*As he comes into the picture, she retreats, walking backwards. Then there is a hoot from the gin. The sound from the gin suddenly stops. This calls her attention to the gin and she starts in that direction.*]

SILVA: Boy.

BOY: Yes, sir.

SILVA: Here's that five dollars the lady was mentioning.

BOY: Yes, sir.

SILVA: Only she don't want you to cut the grass.

BOY: Yes, sir.

SILVA: So you go on like you were. Understand?

BOY: Oh, yes, sir. Thank you, sir. [*The boy, now completely bewildered, goes on, as he was.*]

69]

INTERIOR. COTTON GIN.

[*Something is wrong. The men, including* ROCK, *are gathered around a large piece of machinery. There is the characteristic debate as to what is wrong, opinions differing.*
Onto to this rather hectic group runs BABY DOLL. ARCHIE *turns on her viciously.*]

ARCHIE: What're you doin' here, have you gone crazy??

BABY DOLL: I want to tell you something! You big slob.
[*This is just a little more than a desperate and harassed* ARCHIE *can bear. He suddenly comes across and smacks* BABY DOLL. *Good and hard.*]

ARCHIE: I told you never, never, never, to cross that road to this cotton gin —

70]

CLOSE SHOT. SILVA.
[*He has entered and seen the action.*]

71]

ARCHIE.
[*He notices* SILVA.]

ARCHIE: ... this cotton gin when niggers are working here.

BABY DOLL: You left me ... you know what you left with me over there. . . .
[ARCHIE'S *eye wanders over to* SILVA, *and* BABY DOLL *sees him and clams up.*]

72]

SILVA.
[*He now officially enters the scene.*]

SILVA: How's progress, Mr Meighan?

ARCHIE Fine! Great!

SILVA: Personally, I can't hear the gin at all.

BABY DOLL: [*Full of disgust*] Big Shot! [*And she exits.*]

SILVA: What's holding up?

ARCHIE: Nothing. . . .

SILVA: Rock!
[SILVA'S *own foreman steps forward.*]

ROCK: His saw-cylinder is busted.

SILVA: It figures. I inspected your equipment, Meighan, before I put in my own and I put up my own cotton gin because this equipment was rotten, was rotten, and still is rotten. Now it's quarterpast two by my watch and I counted twenty-three fully loaded wagons still out on your runway. And if you can't move those wagons any faster ...

ARCHIE: Now don't go into any hysterics. You Italians are prone to get too excited. ....

SILVA: Never mind about we Italians. You better get yourself a new saw-cylinder and get this contraption running again. And if you can't get one in Clarksdale, you better go to Tunica, and if you can't get one in Tunica, you better go to Memphis, and if you can't get one in Memphis, keep going to St Louis. Now get on your horse.

ARCHIE: Now listen to me, Silva –

SILVA: One more crack out of you, I'm going to haul across the river. I said get on your horse.

[MEIGHAN *hesitates. Then decides he must swallow this humiliation. There's nothing else for him to do under the circumstances. He exits.*

SILVA *calls* ROCK *over close.*]

SILVA; [*Sotto voce*] I got a saw-cylinder in our commissary. Go get it and bring Hank over to help you put it in. Get this thing running. He ain't gonna get one in Clarksdale, and if he goes to Memphis – well, don't wait for him. [*And he exits.*]

73]

ARCHIE LEE IN HIS CHEVY.
[*He nearly runs* BABY DOLL *over.*]

BABY DOLL: Archie Lee! Archie Lee! Archie Lee! [*She stumbles to her knees. She's sobbing. She rests a moment in the tall grass.*]

74]

SILVA.
[*He runs up to her and stoops down to help her.*]

BABY DOLL: Le' me go. Le' me go. [*She gets up and moves away from him towards her house.*]

AUNT ROSE COMFORT, AND BABY DOLL.

[AUNT ROSE *comes out of the house all dressed up.*]

BABY DOLL: Aunt Rose Comfort.

[AUNT ROSE COMFORT *rushes past her.*]

BABY DOLL: Aunt Rose Comfort!! Where are you going?

AUNT ROSE: I have to see a sick friend at the county hospital.

[*And she is gone.* SILVA *has caught up to* BABY DOLL *again.*]

BABY DOLL: You might as well shout at the moon as that old woman.

SILVA: You didn't want her to go??

BABY DOLL: She's got no business leaving me here alone.

SILVA: It makes you uneasy to be alone here with me.

BABY DOLL: I think she just pretended not to hear me. She has a passion for chocolate candy and she watches the newspapers like a hawk to see if anybody she knows is registered at the county hospital.

SILVA: Hospital . . .?

BABY DOLL: They give candy to patients at the county hospital, friends and relations send them flowers and candy and Aunt Rose Comfort calls on them and eats up their chocolate candy. [SILVA *explodes with laughter.*]

BABY DOLL: One time an old lady friend of Aunt Rose Comfort was dying at the county hospital and Aunt Rose Comfort went over and ate up a two-pound box of chocolate cherries while the old lady was dying, finished it all, hahahaha, while the old lady was dying.

[*They're both laughing together.*]

I like ole people – they're crazy. . . .

[*They both laugh together. . . .*]

SILVA: Mrs Meighan. . . . May I ask you something? Of a personal nature?

BABY DOLL: What?

SILVA: Are you really married to Mr Meighan?

BABY DOLL: Mr Vacarro, that's a personal question.

SILVA: All questions are more or less personal, Mrs Meighan.

BABY DOLL: Well, when I married I wasn't ready for marriage.

I was still eighteen, but my daddy was practically on his death-bed and wanted to see me took care of before he died. Well, ole Archie Lee had been hanging around like a sick dog for quite some time and ... the boys are a sorry lot around here. Ask you to the movies and take you to the old rock quarry instead. You have to get out of the car and throw rocks at 'em, oh, I've had some experiences with boys that would curl your hair if I told you – some – experiences which I've had with boys!! But Archie Lee Meighan was an older fellow and in those days, well, his business was better. You hadn't put up that cotton gin of yours and Archie Lee was ginning out a lot of cotton. You remember?

SILVA: Yes, I remember. ...

BABY DOLL: Well, I told my daddy I wasn't ready for marriage and my daddy told Archie Lee that I wasn't ready for it and he promised my daddy he'd wait till I was ready.

SILVA: Then the marriage was postponed?

BABY DOLL: Not the wedding, no, we had the wedding, my daddy gave me away. ...

SILVA: But you said that Archie Lee waited?

BABY DOLL: Yes, *after* the wedding ... he waited.

SILVA: For what?

BABY DOLL: For me to be ready for marriage.

SILVA: How long did he have to wait?

BABY DOLL: Oh, he's still waiting! Of course, we had an agreement that ... well ... I mean I told him that I'd be ready on my twentieth birthday – I mean ready or *not*. ...

SILVA: And that's tomorrow?

BABY DOLL: Uh-huh.

SILVA: And are you ... will you – be ready?

BABY DOLL: That all depends.

SILVA: What on?

BABY DOLL: Whether or not the furniture comes back – I guess. ...

SILVA: Your husband sweats more than any man I know and now I understand why!!

[*There is a pause. They look at each other. Then* BABY DOLL *looks away. Then with a sudden access of energy she enters the house, slams the screen door in his face and latches it.*]

BABY DOLL: There now! You wait here! You just wait out here!

SILVA: [*Grinning at the screen door*] Yes, ma'am. I will wait.

76]

INTERIOR. DIMLY LIT ENTRANCE HALL OF MEIGHAN HOUSE.

[BABY DOLL *turns from screen door to porch and stumbles along the vast and shadowy hall towards the dim light of the kitchen. As soon as she disappears,* VACARRO *is seen through screen door. He jerks out a pocket-knife and rips a hole in the screen.*

BABY DOLL *calls anxiously, out of sight.*]

BABY DOLL: [*From kitchen*] What's that?

77]

THE PORCH.

[VACARRO *whistles loudly and casually on the porch. He now slips his fingers through the hole and lifts the latch.*]

78]

INTERIOR. KITCHEN OF MEIGHAN HOUSE. FULL SHOT.

[*Large, old-fashioned room with antiquated, but very capacious, equipment – large ice-box, large sinks and draining-boards, large stove converted to gas.*

BABY DOLL *stands in the middle of the floor with an apprehensive expression, but as* VACARRO *continues whistling on the porch, her usual placidity returns. She notices kettle of greens on the stove.*]

BABY DOLL: Stupid old thing – forgot to light the stove. [*She opens the ice-box for lemons.*] Git me a Frigidaire one of these days.

[*The pan under the ice-box has overflowed and is swamping the floor.*]

Got to empty that pan.

[*Pulls it from under refrigerator with a grunt. A sound catches her ear, a sharp, slapping sound. She looks up anxiously, but the sound is not repeated. She takes out lemons, leaves ice-box door banging open. All her movements are fumbling and weak. She keeps rubbing her perspiring hands on her hips. She starts to cut lemon, the knife slips and cuts her finger. She looks at the finger. It looks all right at first, then a drop of blood appears. She whimpers a little. The blood increases. She begins to cry like a baby.*

She makes a vague, anxious movement. Again the slapping sound followed by a soft human sound like a chuckle. She looks that way. Cocks her head. But the sound is not repeated. Still squeezing the cut finger she begins to wander toward the front of the house.

CAMERA PANS WITH BABY DOLL AS SHE WANDERS THROUGH HOUSE.

She passes through a bare huge room with a dusty chandelier. It was the dining-room when the house belonged to the old plantation owners. She whimpers under her breath, squeezing the bleeding finger. Now the blood is running down the hand to the wrist and down the wrist to the forearm and trickling into the soft hollow of her elbow. She groans and whimpers at the sight of the great flight of stairs, but starts up them.

Half-way up, at the landing, she hears the slapping sound again and the faun-like mocking laughter. She stops there and waits and listens – but the sound isn't immediately repeated, so she goes on up. She goes into the bathroom and starts to bandage her cut finger.]

79]

INTERIOR HALL OF MEIGHAN HOUSE.
VACARRO DISCOVERED. FULL SHOT.

[VACARRO *is grinning up at the staircase. He slaps the banisters viciously with his whip, then chuckles.*

CAMERA PANS WITH VACARRO.

He strolls into the kitchen, sees ice-box door hanging open. Helps himself to the remains of a chicken, tearing it apart and gnawing the meat off it. He notices lemons and bloodspots – laughs.]

SILVA: Trail o' blood! Ha ha! [*He empties the flooded ice-pan over dirty dishes in sink.*] Filth! Disgusting! [*He slaps the wall with whip and laughs.*]

80]

INTERIOR. THE MEIGHANS' BEDROOM.
BABY DOLL WANDERS IN FROM BATHROOM.

[*The finger is clumsily bandaged now, and she wanders across the room and examines herself in the mirror.*]

BABY DOLL: Look a' me! Big mess. . . .

[*There are dark stains of sweat on the water-melon pink dress. She lazily starts to remove it. Hears the slapping sound and laugh closer. Pauses, her mouth hanging open. Fumbling attempt to lock door. Key slips from her weak, nerveless fingers. She stoops, grunting, to pick it up.*]

81]

INTERIOR KITCHEN.
VACARRO SQUEEZING LEMONS AND
HURLING THE RINDS SAVAGELY AWAY.

[*He finds gin bottle and sloshes gin into pitcher. Takes ice-pick and chops off big hunk of ice. He seems to enjoy all these physical activities, grins tightly, exposing his teeth. Sticks ice-pick into wall as if he were stabbing an enemy. Holds pitcher over his head whirling it rapidly so the drink sloshes over and ice rattles loudly, liquid running down his bare brown muscular arm. He drinks out of pitcher.*]

82]

INTERIOR BEDROOM. BABY DOLL IN DAMP
SLIP ROOTING IN CLOSET FOR A FRESH
DRESS.

[*She hears ice rattling in pitcher. Pauses. Cocks head, listening apprehensively. Makes sure door is locked.*]

83]

INTERIOR MEIGHANS' BEDROOM –
A DIFFERENT ANGLE. BABY DOLL.

[*Her slip hangs half off one great globular breast, gleaming with sweat. She listens intently.*]

84]

INTERIOR HALL AND STAIRWAY OF
MEIGHAN HOUSE. VACARRO SOFTLY
CLIMBING STAIRS.
CAMERA FOLLOWS VACARRO INTO ROOMS
ACROSS HALL FROM BEDROOM – THEN
INTO CHILD'S NURSERY –

[*Never used. Hobby horse, small fenced bed, Mother Goose pictures on wall. He sits astride wooden horse, lashes its rump with the whip and rocks on it.*]

85]

INTERIOR MEIGHANS' BEDROOM.
BABY DOLL SPRINGS UP FROM FLOOR.

[BABY DOLL *unlocks the door and peers anxiously into hall. The noise stops.*]

BABY DOLL: Archie Lee! Is that you?

[VACARRO (*out of sight*) *gives a soft wolf-whistle.*]

BABY DOLL: Who's that? Who's in there? [*She crosses the hall into nursery.*]

86]

INTERIOR NURSERY. VACARRO SLIPPING
INTO NEXT ROOM AS BABY DOLL ENTERS.

BABY DOLL: [*Nervously*] Hey! What's goin' on?

[*Whip slap and soft mocking laughter, barely audible.*]

BABY DOLL: Mr Vacarro? Are you in that room?

[*She crosses fearfully and enters next room,* VACARRO *slipping out just before her entrance. Now she is really frightened.*]

87]

INTERIOR EMPTY ROOM ADJOINING
NURSERY – FULL SHOT. BABY DOLL
ENTERS FEARFULLY.

BABY DOLL: You! Git outa my house! You got no right to
come in! Where are you?

[*The door to the hall is locked. She hears the key turn in the lock.
Gasps. Pounds door. Rushes back panting into nursery.*]

88]

INTERIOR NURSERY. BABY DOLL RUSHES IN.

BABY DOLL: Mr Vacarro, stop playing hide-and-seek!

[*The soft mocking laughter comes from the hall.*]

I know it's you! You're making me very nervous! Mr
Vacarro!! Mr Vacarro.... Mr Vacarro....

[*With each call she creeps forward a few steps. All of a sudden
he springs at her, shouting –*]

SILVA: [*Sudden shout*] BOO!

[*At this point the scene turns into a wild romp of children. She
shrieks with laughter. He howls, shouts. She shrieks with terror.
She giggles hysterically, running into the hall and starting down
steps. He leaps upon banister and slides to foot of stairs. She
turns on the stairs and runs through various rooms slamming
doors, giggling hysterically as she runs. A spirit of abandon
enters the flight and the pursuit. As he follows her into the
bedroom, she throws a pillow at him. He does a comic pratfall,
embracing the pillow. She shrieks with laughter. He lunges
toward her, throwing the pillow at her fugitive figure.
She is about to run downstairs, but he blocks the way. She
screams and takes the steps to the attic.*]

89]

INTERIOR ATTIC.

[*Dusty late afternoon beams of light through tiny peaked
windows in gables and a jumble of discarded things that have the
poetry of things once lived with by the no-longer living.*

BABY DOLL *doesn't stop to observe all this. She probably didn't even expect to find herself in an attic. She rushes in, slams the door, discovers a rusty bolt and bolts it just as* VACARRO *arrives at the door.*

Her panting laughter expires as he pushes the door. She suddenly realizes the full import of her situation; gasps and backs away.]

SILVA: Open Sesame!!

BABY DOLL: [*In a low, serious voice*] The game is over. I've quit.

SILVA: That's not fair, you've got to keep playing hide-and-seek till you're it.

BABY DOLL: Mr Vacarro, will you please go back downstairs so I can unlock the door of this attic and come out – because the floor is weak.... I don't want to fall through. It's crumbling under my feet. I had no idea – I never been up here before! – it was in such a weaken condition. [*There is something appealing in her soft, pleasing voice.*]

SILVA: [*Whispering, mouth to crack*] I wouldn't dream of leaving you alone in a falling-down attic any more than you'd dream of eatin' a nut a man had cracked in his mouth. Don't you realize that??

BABY DOLL: [*With sudden gathering panic*] Mr Vacarro! I got to get out of here. Quick! Go! Go! – down! Quick, please!

SILVA: I can hear that old floor giving away fast....

BABY DOLL: So can I, and I'm *on* it.

SILVA: Shall I call the fire department to come here with a net to catch you when you fall through?

BABY DOLL: Wouldn't be time. No! Go! – then I can unlock the –

SILVA: No, I don't suppose they'd get here on time or if they did the net would be rotten as those fire hoses last night when they came to put out the fire that burned down my gin!

[*Suddenly, a piece of plaster falls beneath her feet. The rotten laths are exposed. She scrambles to another place, which is – or seems – equally shaky. She screams.*]

SILVA: Are you being attacked by a ghost in there?

BABY DOLL: Please be kind! Go away!

SILVA: Why don't you unlock the door so I can come to your rescue?

BABY DOLL: I – can't because ...

SILVA: Huh? Huh?

BABY DOLL: [*Whisper*] YOU.

[VACARRO *shoves door just a little with his shoulder. The bolt is not strong.*]

You ... so! *Scare* me!

SILVA: Scared of *me*??

BABY DOLL: Yeah, scared of you and your – *whip*.

SILVA: Why're you scared of my whip? Huh? Do you think I might whip you? Huh? Scared I might whip you with it and

[*Slaps boots regularly with riding crop.*]

leave red marks on your – body, on your – creamy white silk – skin? Is that why're scared, Mrs Meighan?

[*A murmur from her.*]

You want me to go away – with my whip??

[*Another murmur.*]

All right. Tell you what I'm gonna do. I'm gonna slip pencil and paper under this door and all I want is your signature on the paper....

BABY DOLL: What paper?

SILVA: I guess that you would call it an affidavit, legally stating that Archie Lee Meighan burned down the Syndicate Gin.... [*Pause*] Okay?

BABY DOLL: Mr Vacarro, this whole floor's about to collapse under me!

SILVA: What do you say?

BABY DOLL: Just leave the paper, leave it right out there and I'll sign it and send it to you, I'll ...

SILVA: Mrs Meighan, I am a Sicilian. They're an old race of people, an ancient race, and ancient races aren't trustful races by nature. I've got to have the signed paper now. Otherwise I'm going to break this door down. Do you hear me? [*A pause*] Do you hear me?

[*Silence*]

[*Whimpering, sobbing.*] I gather you don't believe me.

[*Suddenly, with a single eloquent gesture of his whole body he has pushed the door open and on the other side* BABY DOLL, *in absolute panic, runs, runs away from the threatening man and whip and towards the darkest corner of the attic. A few steps, however, and the floor really gives way. There is a shower of plaster, a rising cloud of plaster dust.*

VACARRO'S *face.*

The dust settles to reveal her, precariously perched across a beam ...

VACARRO *calmly lights a cigarette.*]

SILVA: Now you're either going to agree to sign this thing, or I'm going to come out there after you and my additional weight will make the whole floor you know what!

BABY DOLL: OOOOOOH! What am I gonna do?

SILVA: Do what I tell you. [*He gingerly steps on a place.... A trickle of plaster*] Awful bad shape.

[*He reaches and picks up a 1 × 3 about twelve feet long. On the end of it he puts a pencil and piece of paper.*]

BABY DOLL: O-o-o-o-o-h!

SILVA: What? [*Suddenly, he stamps on the plaster. There is a big fall of plaster;* BABY DOLL *screams.*]

BABY DOLL: All right, all right. – All right.... Hurry! Hurry!

SILVA: Hurry what?

BABY DOLL: I'll do whatever you want – only hurry!!

SILVA: Here it comes....

[*He reaches out his little piece of paper and pencil, balanced on the 1 × 3. She grabs it, scribbles her name in frantic haste, panting, and puts the piece of paper back, fixing it on a nail on the end of the 1 × 3, and* VACARRO *pulls it back. He looks at her signature and throws back his head in a sudden wild laugh.*]

SILVA: Thank you. You may come out now.

BABY DOLL: Not till I hear you! Going down those stairs. ...

SILVA: [*Grinning and starting down*] Hear me? Hear my descending footsteps on the stairs. ...

[VACARRO *straddles the long spiralled banister and slides all*

the way down to the landing at the bottom with a leap that starts
another minor cascade.

BABY DOLL *utters a little cry and comes out of the attic door.*
Silence. Putt-putt-putt-putt of the gin. She leans over stair well
and looks straight down into the grinning face of VACARRO.
He gives her a quick, grinning nod or salute.]

SILVA: Okay, you're 'Home free'! And so am I! Bye-bye!

BABY DOLL: Where are you going??

SILVA: Back to my little grey Quonset home in the West! For
a peaceful siesta. . . .

BABY DOLL: Wait, please! – I want to –
[*She starts to come running down the stairs, her hair wild,*
panting, sweating, smeared with attic dust. Then half-way down
she stops. . . .]

BABY DOLL: [*Now stealing towards him*] I want to –
[*But she can't remember what she 'wants to'. He waits quizzi-*
cally with his cocky grin for her to complete her sentence but she
doesn't. Instead she looks up and down him and her eyelids
flutter as if the image could not be quietly contained.
He nods as if in agreement to something stated. He chuckles and
then turns on his heels and starts briskly for the porch. She calls
after him . . .]

BABY DOLL: Was *that* all you wanted . . .?
[*He turns and looks at her.*]
Me to confess that Archie Lee burnt down your gin?

SILVA: What else did you imagine?
[*She turns away like a shy child, serious-faced; she sits down on*
the bottom step.]

SILVA: [*Gently*] You're a child, Mrs Meighan. That's why we
played hide-and-seek, a game for children. . . .

BABY DOLL: You don't have to go all the way to your place
for a nap. You could take a nap here.

SILVA: But all the furniture's been removed from the house.

BABY DOLL: Not the nursery stuff. They's a small bed in
there, a crib, you could curl up and – let the slats down. . . .
[*An effect of two shy children trying to strike up a friendship.*
He continues to look at her. The windy afternoon has tossed a
cloud over the sun, now declining. But it passes and his smile

68

becomes as warm as sunlight. She isn't looking into his face but down at the scuffed kid slippers. Abruptly he gives a short quick nod and says simply . . .

SILVA: I'm happy to accept the invitation. [*He starts up the stairs. When he gets to the point where she is sitting, he says*] Come up and sing me to sleep. [*Then he continues on up*]
  [BABY DOLL *is left alone, bewildered, sitting alone on the big staircase.*]

BABY DOLL: [*To herself*] My daddy would *turn* in his *grave*. [*She starts up the stairs. . . .*]

90]

THE NURSERY.
  [VACARRO *is on the crib, with the slats down. He is curled with his thumb in his mouth. She comes to view, stands in the doorway a moment, then goes and crouches beside the bed. Gently, she raises his head and bare throat, crooks an arm under and begins to sing, 'Rock-a-Bye Baby'.*
  He sighs contentedly, removes the signed paper from his shirt pocket and tucks it under his belt for safer keeping.
  Then he appears to fall asleep.]

DISSOLVE.

91]

IN A HOSPITAL ROOM.
  [AUNT ROSE COMFORT *is sitting by a friend who is in her death coma.* AUNT ROSE *eating chocolate cherries.*]

DISSOLVE.

92]

SUPPLY STORE IN MEMPHIS. MEIGHAN AT COUNTER.

ARCHIE: [*To clerk*] Godamighty, man, I'm good for it.
  [*He reaches for the part he has come for. It's wrapped and ready to go.*]

CLERK: We have orders. No credit. Cash basis. Everything.

ARCHIE: I warn you. I'll never come in this store again.
CLERK: Sorry.
ARCHIE: Look, I just happened to leave the place in my work
clothes. My wallet ain't on me!
CLERK: Cash only.
   [MR ARCHIE LEE MEIGHAN *suddenly turns and leaves in*
   complete disgust.]

93]

FRONT. ARCHIE LEE'S GIN.
   [*It is several hours later and he has driven back from Memphis.*
   He halts his motor with an exhausted grunt. He appears to have
   shrunk in size. He carries a sweat-drenched coat over his arm and
   the sweaty shirt clings to him. His chest heaves with unhealthy
   fast respiration, and he fingers the unbuttoned collar, as he takes
   in the situation. The gin is running again!!! – and without his
   O.K. – and how did they get the damned thing going again!!??]

93A]

INTERIOR GIN.
   [*He walks in and passes* ROCK.]
ARCHIE: Hahaha! Looks like we're back in business.
ROCK: [*Offers him only the most fleeting glance*] Does, doesn't it.
ARCHIE: You all must have done some mighty fast repairs.
ROCK: No repairs – put in a new saw-cylinder.
ARCHIE: From where? Out of a cloud? Why, I checked every
supply outfit between Memphis and Greenville and no-
body's got a new saw-cylinder ready for installation before
next Wednesday.
ROCK: [*Tersely*] Boss had one at our place. I put it in.
ARCHIE: How do you like that? How come I wasn't let in on
this piece of information before I lit out of here on the
wild-goose chase that just about killed me? Where is that
wop Vacarro? I want to get some explanation of this.
   [*At this precise moment the whistle blows, announcing the end of*
   the day and the gin machinery stops work. The Negroes, who
   have been working as porters and mechanics, line up for pay.]

ROCK: [*Meantime*] You seen the boss-man, Norm?
[*A Negro shakes his head.*
ROCK *notices* ARCHIE *looking at the line a little worried.*]
ROCK: [*To* ARCHIE] Don't worry. Vacarro is meeting the pay-roll for tonight.
ARCHIE: Where is he?
ROCK: [*To another Negro*] Moose, you seen the boss?
MOOSE: No time lately, Capt'n.

94]

THE GIN. (ANOTHER ANGLE)
[MEIGHAN *retreats from the gin uncertainly. Camera follows. Half-way across the road he hears laughter, evidently directed at him. His back stiffens. Something has happened, he feels, that has somehow made him the patsy of whatever occasion this is.*]

95]

CLOSE SHOT. MEIGHAN.
[*Suspicious, angry, something violent and dangerous is growing up in his heart. He mutters to himself. Hears the laughter again. Curses to himself.*]

96]

MEIGHAN ENTERS THE BIG FRONT YARD AND STARES AT THE HOUSE.

97]

THE HOUSE.
[*Silent. Not a move. Not a sound.*]

98]

MEIGHAN NOTICES VACARRO'S DISCARDED SHIRT.
[*He picks it up and lifts his head and calls into the house.*]

ARCHIE: Hey! Anybody living here? Anybody still living in this house?

99]

UPSTAIRS. THE NURSERY.

[BABY DOLL, *considerably disarrayed, has heard* ARCHIE's *shout from below and is just making her way on hands and knees to the window. Now she crawls on the floor over to the crib.*]

BABY DOLL: It's Archie Lee.

[*Downstairs screen door slams.* VACARRO *gurgles, murmurs, whimpers, all of which mean 'don't bother me, I want to sleep'. There is a sudden shout from downstairs as if a cry of pain.*]

100]

DOWNSTAIRS.

[*What* MEIGHAN *sees is the debris of the ceiling. He looks up at the gaping hole in the roof over his head at the top of the stair well and then down the stairs.* BABY DOLL *appears on the staircase in a silken wrapper.*]

ARCHIE: *What happened here?*

[BABY DOLL *doesn't answer. She stares at him with blank insolence.*]

ARCHIE: Hunh? I said what the hell happened here?

BABY DOLL: You mean that mess in the ·hall? The plaster broke in the attic.

ARCHIE: How'd that – how'd that – happen?

BABY DOLL: How does anything happen? It just happened.

[*She comes on lazily down, avoiding his look.*]

101]

INTERIOR NIGHT. DOWNSTAIRS. FRONT HALL.

ARCHIE: Ain't I told you not to slop around here in a slip?

[*She gives a faint indifferent shrug which enrages him; he senses something openly contemptuous, a change in her attitude towards him. He grabs her bare shoulder.*]

What's the matter with your skin? It looks all broke out. [*Inspects the inflamed welts*] What's this?

BABY DOLL: What's what?

ARCHIE: These marks on you?

BABY DOLL: Mosquito bites, I scratched them. . . . Lemme go.

ARCHIE: [*Bellowing*] Ain't I told you not to slop around here in a slip???!!!

[AUNT ROSE COMFORT, *alarmed by the shout, appears in door to kitchen, crying out thin and high.*]

AUNT ROSE: Almost ready, now, folks, almost ready!!

[*She rushes back into the kitchen with her frightened cackle. There is a crash of china from the kitchen.*]

ARCHIE: The breakage alone in that kitchen would ruin a well-to-do-man! Now you go up and git some decent clo'se on yuh an' come back down. Y'know they got a new bureau in Washington, D.C. It's called the U.W. Bureau. Y'know what U.W. stands for? It stands fo' useless women. They's secret plans on foot to round 'em all up and shoot 'em. Hahahaha!

BABY DOLL: How about men that's destructive? Don't they have secret plans to round up men that's destructive and shoot them too?

ARCHIE: What destructive men you talkin' about?

BABY DOLL: Men that blow things up and burn things down because they're too evil and stupid to git along otherwise. Because fair competition is too much for 'em. So they turn criminal. Do things like Arson. Wilful destruction of property by fire. . . . [*She steps out on the porch. Night sounds. A cool breeze tosses her damp curls. She sniffs the night air like a young horse. . . . The porch light, a milky globe patterned with dead insects, turns on directly over her head and* ARCHIE LEE *comes up behind her and grips her bare shoulders, his face anxious, cunning.*]

ARCHIE: Who said that to you? Where'd you git that from??

BABY DOLL: Turn that porch light off. There's men on the road can see me.

ARCHIE: Who said *arson* to you? Who spoke of wilful destruction of ... YOU never knew them words. Who SAID 'em to yuh?

BABY DOLL: Sometimes, Big Shot, you don't seem t' give me credit for much intelligence! I've been to school, in my life, and I'm a – magazine reader!

[*She shakes off his grip and starts down porch steps. There is a group of men on Tiger Tail Road. One of them gives a wolf-whistle. At once, ARCHIE LEE charges down the steps and across the yard towards the road – crying out –*

ARCHIE: *Who gave that whistle??* Which of you give a wolf-whistle at my wife?

[*The group ignores him except for a light mocking laugh as they continue down road. The Camera returns to* BABY DOLL *blandly smiling.*

We hear the rattle of the cistern pump being vigorously exercised in the side yard. ARCHIE LEE *stalks back up to porch, winded, like an old hound....*]

ARCHIE: Men from the Syndicate *Plantation! White an' black* mixed! Headed fo' Tiger Tail Bayou with frog gigs and rubber boots on! I just hope they turn downstream and trespass across my property! I just hope they dast to! I'll blast them out of the Bayou with a shotgun!

BABY DOLL: Small dogs have a loud bark.

ARCHIE: Nobody's gonna insult no woman of *mine*!!

BABY DOLL: You take a lot for granted when you say *mine.* This afternoon I come to you for protection. What did I *git? Slapped!* And told to go home.... I, for one, have got no sympathy for you, now or ever. An' the rasslin' match between us is *over* so let me *go*!

ARCHIE: You're darn tootin' it's over. In just three hours the terms of the agreement will be settled for good.

BABY DOLL: Don't count on it. That agreement is cancelled. Because it takes two sides to make an agreement, like an argument, and both sides got to live up to it completely. You didn't live up to yours. Stuck me in a house which is haunted and five complete sets of unpaid-for furniture was removed from it las' night, OOHH I'm *free* from my side of that bargain!

ARCHIE: *Sharp at midnight!* We'll find out about that.

BABY DOLL: Too much has happened here lately. . . .

[*She descends into yard.* ARCHIE LEE *eyes her figure, sweating, licking his chops.*]

ARCHIE: Well . . . my credit's wide open again!

BABY DOLL: So is the jail-house door wide open for you if the truth comes out.

ARCHIE: You threatenin' me with – *blackmail*??

BABY DOLL: Somebody's drawin' some cool well water from the pump back there.

[*She starts back. He follows. The full frog-gigging moon emerges from a mackerel sky, and we see* VACARRO *making his ablutions at the cistern pump with the zest and vigour of a man satisfied.*]

BABY DOLL: [*With unaccustomed hilarity*] HEIGH-HO SILVER . . . HaHa!!

[ARCHIE LEE *stops dead in his tracks.*]

ARCHIE: Him?! Still on the place?

BABY DOLL: Give me another drink of that sweet well water, will yuh, Mistuh Vacarro? You're the first person could draw it.

ARCHIE: [*Advancing*] YOU STILL HERE?

BABY DOLL: Archie Lee, Mr Vacarro says he might not put up a new cotton gin, but let you gin cotton for him all the time, now. Ain't you pleased about that? Tomorrow he plans to come with lots more cotton, maybe another twenty-seven wagon-loads. And while you're ginning it out, he'll have me entertain him, make lemonade for him. It's going to go on and on! Maybe even next fall.

SILVA: [*Through the water*] Good neighbour policy in practice. [*Having wetted himself down he now drinks from gourd*] I love well water. It tastes as fresh as if it never was tasted before. Mrs Meighan, would you care for some, too?

BABY DOLL: Why thank you, yes, I would. [*There is a grace and sweetness and softness of speech about her, unknown before. . . .*]

SILVA: Cooler nights have begun.

[ARCHIE LEE *has been regarding the situation, with its various possibilities, and is far from content.*]

ARCHIE: How long you been on the place?

SILVA: [*Drawling sensuously with eyes on girl*] All this unusually long hot fall afternoon I've imposed on your hospitality. You want some of this well water?

ARCHIE: [*With a violent gesture of refusal*] Where you been here???

SILVA: Taking a nap on your only remaining bed. The crib in the nursery with the slats let down. I had to curl up on it like a pretzel, but the fire last night deprived me of so much sleep that almost any flat surface was suitable for slumber.

[*Winks impertinently at* ARCHIE LEE, *then turns to grin sweetly at* BABY DOLL, *wiping the drippings of well water from his throat. Then turns back to* ARCHIE]

But there's something sad about it. Know what I mean?

ARCHIE: Sad about what??

SILVA: An unoccupied nursery in a house, and all the other rooms empty....

ARCHIE: That's no problem of yours!

SILVA: The good-neighbour policy makes your problems mine – and vice versa....

AUNT ROSE: [*Violent and high and shrill, from the back steps*] SUPPER! READY! CHILDREN.... [*She staggers back in.*]

[*Now there's a pause in which all three stand tense and silent about the water pump.* BABY DOLL *with her slow, new smile speaks up first....*]

BABY DOLL: You all didn't hear us called in to supper?

ARCHIE: You gonna eat here tonight?

SILVA: Mrs Meighan asked me to stay for supper but I told her I'd better get to hear the invitation from the head of the house before I'd feel free to accept it. So ... What do you say?

[*A tense pause ... then, with great difficulty ...*]

ARCHIE: Stay! ... fo' supper.

BABY DOLL: You'll have to take pot luck.

SILVA: I wouldn't be putting you out?

[*This is addressed to* BABY DOLL, *who smiles vaguely and starts toward the house, saying* . . .]

BABY DOLL: I better get into mu' clo'se. . . .

ARCHIE: Yeah . . . hunh. . . .

[*They follow her sensuous departure with their eyes till she fades into the dusk.*]

ARCHIE: Did I understand you to say you wouldn't build a new gin but would leave your business to me?

SILVA: If that's agreeable with you. . . .

ARCHIE: [*Turning from his wife's back to* VACARRO's *face*] I don't know yet, I'll have to consider the matter. . . . Financing is involved such as – new equipment. . . . Let's go in and eat now. I got a pain in my belly, I got a sort of heartburn. . . .

102]

INTERIOR HOUSE.

[*They enter the kitchen and then to the dining-room.* ARCHIE LEE's *condition is almost shock. He can't quite get with the situation. He numbly figures that he'd better play it cool till the inner fog clears. But his instinct is murder. His cowardly caution focuses his malice on the old woman and the unsatisfactory supper she's prepared.*]

ARCHIE: Hey! Hey! One more place at the table! Mr Vacarro from the Syndicate Plantation is stayin' to supper.

AUNT ROSE: [*With a startled outcry, clutching her chest*] Oh – I had no idea that company was expected. Just let me – change the silver and . . .

ARCHIE: Another place is all that's called for. Have you been here all day?

AUNT ROSE: What was that, Archie Lee?

ARCHIE: HAVE YOU BEEN IN THE HOUSE ALL AFTERNOON OR DID YOU LIGHT OUT TO THE COUNTY HOSPITAL TO EAT SOME CHOCOLATE CANDY????

[AUNT ROSE *gasps as if struck, then she cackles* . . .]

AUNT ROSE: I – I – visited! – an old friend in a – coma!

77

ARCHIE: Then you was out while I was – . [*Turns to* VACARRO – *fiercely*] I work like the hammers of hell! I come home to find the attic floor fell through, my wife bad-tempered, insulting! and a supper of hog slops – . Sit down, eat. I got to make a phone call.

[*He crosses somewhat unsteadily into the hall and picks up the telephone as* BABY DOLL *descends the grand staircase and goes past him with her face austerely averted. She is clad in a fresh silk sheath and is adjusting an earring as she passes through the hall. We go with her into dining-room.*]

BABY DOLL: He's at the phone about something and if I was you, I wouldn't hang around long.

SILVA: I think I've got the ace of spades in my pocket. [*He pats where he's stashed the confession signed by* BABY DOLL.]

BABY DOLL: Don't count on a law court. Justice is deaf and blind as that old woman!

[AUNT ROSE COMFORT *rushes out to cut roses for a vase to set on table.*]

BABY DOLL: I'm advising you, go! – while he's on the phone.

SILVA: I find you different this evening in some way.

BABY DOLL: Never mind, just go! Before he gits off the phone.

SILVA: Suddenly grown up!

BABY DOLL: [*Looking at him gratefully*] I feel cool and rested, for the first time in my life. I feel that way, rested and cool. [*A pause*] Are you going or staying???

[*They are close together by table. Suddenly she catches her breath and flattens her body to his. The embrace is active. She reaches above her and pulls the beaded chain of the light bulb, plunging the room in dark. We hear two things, the breath of the embracing couple and the voice of* ARCHIE LEE *on the phone.*]

ARCHIE: A bunch of men from the Syndicate Plantation are out frog-giggin' on Tiger Tail Bayou and I thought we all might join the party. How's about meeting at the Brite Spot in halfn hour? With full equipment.

[*A few more indistinct words, he hangs up. The light is switched back on in the dining-room.* AUNT ROSE *rushes in.*]

AUNT ROSE: Roses! Poems of nature ...

[ARCHIE LEE *enters from the hall. His agitation is steadily mounting.*]

ARCHIE: Never mind poems of nature, just put food on th' table!

AUNT ROSE: If I'd only known that company was expected, I'd ... [*Her breathless voice expires as she scuttles about putting roses in a vase.*]

AUNT ROSE: Only take a minute.

ARCHIE: We ain't waitin' no minute. Bring out the food....
[BABY DOLL *smiles, rather scornfully, at* ARCHIE LEE *bullying the old woman.*]

ARCHIE: Is that what they call a Mona Lisa smile you got on your puss?

BABY DOLL: Don't pick on Aunt Rose....

ARCHIE: [*Shouting*] Put some food on the table!! [*Then muttering dangerously*] I'm going to have a talk with that old woman, right here tonight. She's outstayed her welcome.

SILVA: What a pretty blue wrapper you're wearing tonight, Mrs Meighan.

BABY DOLL: [*Coyly*] Thank you, Mr Vacarro.

SILVA: There's so many shades of blue. Which shade is that?

BABY DOLL: Just baby blue.

ARCHIE: Baby blue, huh!

SILVA: It brings out the blue of your eyes.

ARCHIE: [*Screaming*] Food! Food!

AUNT ROSE: Immediately! This instant!
[*She comes through door from the kitchen, holding a big plate of greens, which she sets on the table with great apprehension. They are not really cooked.* ARCHIE *stares at them.*]

103]

CLOSE SHOT OF GREENS, WHICH ARE ALMOST RAW.

104]

CLOSE SHOT OF ARCHIE SWEARING UNDER HIS BREATH.

105]

GROUP SCENE.

BABY DOLL: This wrapper was part of my trousseau, as a matter of fact. I got all my trousseau at Memphis at various departments where my daddy was known. Big department stores on Main Street.

ARCHIE: WHAT IS THIS STUFF??!! GRASS??!!

BABY DOLL: Greens! Don't you know greens when you see them?

ARCHIE: This stuff is greens??!!

[AUNT ROSE *comes nervously from pantry.*]

AUNT ROSE: Archie Lee dotes on greens, don't you, Archie Lee?

ARCHIE: No, I don't.

AUNT ROSE: You don't? You don't dote on greens?

ARCHIE: I don't think I ever declared any terrible fondness for greens in your presence.

AUNT ROSE: Well, somebody did.

ARCHIE: Somebody probably did – sometime, somewhere, but that don't mean it was me!

[*Lurches back in his chair and half rises, swinging to face* VACARRO–*who had taken* BABY DOLL's *hand under the table.* VACARRO *smiles blandly.*]

BABY DOLL: Sit back down, Big Shot, an' eat your greens. Greens put iron in the system.

AUNT ROSE: I thought that Archie Lee doted on greens! – All those likes an' dislikes are hard to keep straight in your head. But Archie Lee's easy to cook for. Jim's a complainer, oh, my, what a complainer Jim is, and Susie's household, they're nothing but complainers.

ARCHIE: *Take this slop off th' table!!*

AUNT ROSE: [*Terrified*] I'll – cook you some – eggs Birmingham! – These greens didn' cook long enough. I played a fool trick with my stove. I forgot to light it! Ha ha! When I went out to the store – I had my greens on the stove. I thought I'd left 'em boilin'. But when I got home I discovered that my stove wasn't lighted.

ARCHIE: Why do you say 'my' stove? Why is everything 'my'?

BABY DOLL: Archie Lee, I believe you been drinkin'!

ARCHIE: You keep out of this! Set down, Aunt Rose.

AUNT ROSE: – Do what, Archie Lee?

ARCHIE: Set down here. I want to ask you a question.

[AUNT ROSE *sits down slowly and stiffly, all a-tremble.*] What sort of – plans have you made?

AUNT ROSE: Plans, Archie Lee? What sort of plans do you mean?

ARCHIE: Plans for the future!

BABY DOLL: I don't think this kind of discussion is necessary in front of company.

SILVA: Mr Meighan, when a man is feeling uncomfortable over something, it often happens that he takes out his annoyance on some completely innocent person just because he has to make somebody suffer.

ARCHIE: You keep outa this, too. I'm askin' Aunt Rose a perfectly sensible question. Now, Aunt Rose. You been here since August and that's a mighty long stay. Now, it's my honest opinion that you're in need of a rest. You been cookin' around here and cooking' around there for how long now? How long have you been cookin' around people's houses?

AUNT ROSE: [*Barely able to speak*] I've helped out my – relatives, my – folks – whenever they – *needed me to*! I was always – *invited*! Sometimes – *begged* to come! When *babies* were expected or when somebody was *sick*, they called for Aunt Rose, and Aunt Rose was always – ready.... Nobody *ever* had to – *put me – out*! If you – gentlemen will excuse me from the table – I will pack my things! If I hurry I'll catch the nine o'clock bus to –

[*She can't think 'where to'.* VACARRO *seizes her hand, pushing back from table.*]

SILVA: Miss Rose Comfort. Wait. I'll drive you home.

AUNT ROSE: – I don't! – have nowhere to! – go....

SILVA: Yes, you do. I need someone to cook for me at my place. I'm tired of my own cooking and I am anxious to try those eggs Birmingham you mentioned. Is it a deal?

AUNT ROSE: – Why, I –

BABY DOLL: Sure it's a deal. Mr Vacarro will be good to you, Aunt Rose Comfort, and he will even *pay* you, and maybe – well – y'never can tell about things in the future. ...

AUNT ROSE: *I'll run pack my things!*
[*She resumes reedy hymn in a breathless, cracked voice as she goes upstairs.*]

ARCHIE: Anything else around here you wanta take with yuh, Vacarro?

SILVA:
[*Looks around coolly as if considering the question*]

BABY DOLL:
[*Utters a high, childish giggle*]

ARCHIE: Well, *is* they? Anything else around here you wanta take away with yuh?

BABY DOLL: [*Rising gaily*] Why, yaiss, Archie Lee. Mr Vacarro noticed the house was overloaded with furniture and he would like us to loan him five complete sets of it to –

ARCHIE: [*Seizing neck of whiskey bottle*] YOU SHUDDUP! I will git to you later.

BABY DOLL: If you ever git to me it sure is going to be *later*, ha, ha, *much* later, ha ha!
[*She crosses to kitchen sink, arranging her kiss-me-quicks in the soap-splashed mirror, also regarding the two men behind her with bland satisfaction; her childish face, beaming, is distorted by the flared glass.*
She sings or hums 'Sweet and Lovely'. ARCHIE LEE *stands by table, breathing heavy as a walrus in labour. He looks from one to the other.* SILVA *coolly picks up a big kitchen knife and lops off a hunk of bread, then tosses kitchen knife out of* ARCHIE LEE'*s reach and then he dips bread in pot of greens.*]

SILVA: Coloured folks call this pot liquor.

BABY DOLL: I love pot liquor.

SILVA: Me, too.

BABY DOLL: [*Dreamily*] – Crazy 'bout pot liquor. ...
[*She turns about and rests her hips against sink.* ARCHIE

LEE's *breathing is loud as a cotton gin, his face fiery. He takes swallow after swallow from bottle.*

VACARRO *devours bread.*]

SILVA: Mm-ummm!

BABY DOLL: Good?

SILVA: *Yes! – Good!*

BABY DOLL: – *That's good. . . .*

[OLD FUSSY *makes a slow stately entrance, pushing the door open wider with her fat hips and squawking peevishly at this slight inconvenience.*

MEIGHAN *wheels about violently and hurls empty bottle at her. She flaps and squawks back out. Her distressed outcries are taken up by her sisters, who are sensibly roosting.*]

BABY DOLL: [*Giggling*] Law! Ole Fussy mighty near made it that time! Why, that old hen was comin' in like she'd been invited t'supper.

[*Her giggly voice expires as* MEIGHAN *wheels back around and bellows.*

ARCHIE LEE *explodes volcanically. His violence should give him almost a Dostoevskian stature.*

It builds steadily through scene as a virtual lunacy possesses him with realization of his hopeless position.]

ARCHIE: OH HO HO HO HO! [*Kicks kitchen door shut*] Now you all listen to me! Quit giving looks back an' forth an' listen to me! Y'think I'm deaf, dumb an' blind, or somethin', do yuh? You're *mistook.* Oh, brother, but you're much, much – *mistook!* Ohhhh, I knooow! – I guess I look like a – I guess I look like a – [*Panting, puffing pause; he reels a little, clutching chair back.*]

BABY DOLL: [*Insolently childish lisp*] What d'you guess you look like, Archie Lee? Y'was about t' tell us an' then yuh quit fo' some –

ARCHIE: *Yeah, yeah, yeah!* Some little innocent Baby Doll of a wife not ready fo' marriage, oh, no, not yet ready for marriage but plenty ready t'– Oh, I see how it's funny, I can see how it's funny, I see the funny side of it. *Oh ho ho ho ho!* Yes, it sure is comic, comic as hell! But there's one little *teensy-eensy* little – thing that you – *overlooked!* I! Got

position! Yeah, yeah, *I* got *position*! Here in this county!
Where I was bo'n an' brought up! I hold a respected
position, lifelong! – member of – Wait! Wait! – Baby
Doll. . . .

[*She had started to cross past him; he seizes her wrist. She
wrenches free.* VACARRO *stirs and tenses slightly but doesn't
rise or change his cool smile.*]

On my side 're friends, long-standin' *bus'ness* associates, an'
social! See what I mean? You ain't got that advantage, have
you, mister? Huh, mister? Ain't you a dago, or something,
excuse me, I mean Eyetalian or something, here in Tiger
Tail County?

SILVA: Meighan, I'm not a doctor, but I was a medical corps-
man in the Navy and you've got a very unhealthy looking
flush on your face right now which is almost purple as a –
[*He was going to say 'baboon's behind'*.]

ARCHIE: [*Bellowing out*] ALL I GOT TO DO IS GIT ON THAT
PHONE IN THE HALL!

SILVA: And call an ambulance from the county hospital?

ARCHIE: Hell, I don't even need t' make a phone call! I can
handle this situation *m'self*! – with legal protection that no
one could –

SILVA: [*Still coolly*] What situation do you mean, Meighan?

ARCHIE: Situation which I come home to find here under my
roof! Oh, I'm not such a marble-missing old fool! – I
couldn't size it up! – I sized it up the moment I seen you
was still on this place and *her*! – with that *sly smile on her*!
[*Takes a great swallow of liquor from the fresh bottle*] And *you*
with *yours* on *you*! I know how to wipe off both of those
sly – !

[*Crosses to closet door.* BABY DOLL *utters a gasp and signals*
VACARRO *to watch out.*]

SILVA: Meighan? [*He speaks coolly, almost with a note of sympathy*] *You* know, and *I* know, and I *know* that you *know*
that I *know*! – That you set fire to my cotton gin last night.
You burnt down the Syndicate Gin and I got in my pocket
a signed affidavit, a paper, signed by a witness, whose
testimony will even hold up in the law courts of Tiger Tail

County! – That's all I come here for and that's all I got . . .
whatever else you suspect – well! you're mistaken. . . . Isn't
that so, Mrs Meighan? Isn't your husband mistaken in
thinking that I got anything out of this place but this
signed affidavit which was the purpose of my all-afternoon
call?

[*She looks at him, angry, hurt.*

MEIGHAN *wheels about, panting.*]

SILVA: [*Continuing*] Yes, I'm foreign but I'm not revengeful,
Meighan, at least not more than is rightful. [*Smiles sweetly*]
– I think we got a workable good-neighbour policy between
us. It might work out, anyhow I think it deserves a try.
Now as to the other side of the situation, which I don't have
to mention. Well, all I can say is, a certain attraction –
exists! Mutually, I believe! But nothing's been rushed. I
needed a little shut-eye after last night's – excitement. I
took a nap upstairs in the nursery crib with the slats let
down to accommodate my fairly small frame, and I have
faint recollection of being sung to by someone – a lullaby
song that was – sweet . . . [*His voice is low, caressing*] – and the
touch of – cool fingers, but that's all, absolutely!

ARCHIE: Y'think I'm gonna put up with this – ?

SILVA: Situation? You went to a whole lot of risk an'
trouble to get my business back. Now don't you want it?
It's up to you, Archie Lee, it's –

ARCHIE: COOL! Yeah, cool, very cool!

SILVA: – The heat of the fire's died down. . . .

ARCHIE: UH – HUH! YOU'VE FIXED YOUR WAGON WITH
THIS SMART TALK, YOU JUST NOW FIXED YOUR
WAGON! I'M GONNA MAKE A PHONE CALL THAT'LL
WIPE THE GRIN OFF YOUR GREASY WOP FACE FOR
GOOD! [*He charges into hall and seizes phone.*]

SILVA: [*Crossing to* BABY DOLL *at kitchen sink*] Is my wop face
greasy, Mrs Meighan?

[*She remains at mirror but her childish smile fades; her face goes
vacant and blind; she suddenly tilts her head back against the bare
throat of the man standing behind her. Her eyes clenched shut. . . .
His eyelids flutter as his body presses against all the mindless*

virgin softness of her abundant young flesh. We can't see their hands, but hers are stretched behind her, his before him.]

106]

HALL.

ARCHIE: [*Bellowing like a steer*] I WANT SPOT, MIZZ HOPKINS, WHE' IS SPOT!?

107]

BABY DOLL WITH VACARRO.

BABY DOLL: I think you better go 'way....

SILVA: I'm just waiting to take you girls away with me....

BABY DOLL: [*Softly as in a dream*] Yeah. I'm goin' too. I'll check in at the Kotton King Hotel and – Now I better go up an' – he'p Aunt Rose Comfo't pack....

[*Releases herself regretfully from the embrace and crosses into hall.*]

108]

HALL. CLOSE SHOT OF SILVA LOOKING AFTER HER. IN THE HALL SHE UTTERS A SHARP OUTCRY AS MEIGHAN STRIKES AT HER.

BABY DOLL: YOU GONNA BE SORRY FOR EV'RY TIME YOU LAID YOUR UGLY OLE HANDS ON ME, YOU STINKER, YOU! YOU STINKING STINKER, STINKERRR!

[*Her footsteps running upstairs.* VACARRO *chuckles almost silently and goes quietly out the back door.*]

109]

THE YARD.

[VACARRO *crosses through a yard littered with uncollected garbage, tin cans, refuse....*]

110]

HALL. MEIGHAN REMOVES SHOTGUN FROM CLOSET.

111]

YARD. CUT BACK TO EXTERIOR.
[*Crooked moon beams fitfully through a racing mackerel sky, the air full of motion.*
VACARRO *picks his way fastidiously among the refuse, wades through the tall seeding grass, into the front yard. Clutches the lower branch of a pecan tree and swings up into it. Cracks a nut between his teeth as –*]
ARCHIE: [*Shouting and blundering through the house*] HEY! WHERE YOU HIDING? WHERE YOU HIDING, WOP?!

112]

HOUSE. CLOSE SHOT OF MEIGHAN WITH SHOTGUN AND LIQUOR BOTTLE, ALREADY STUMBLING DRUNK....

113]

YARD. EXTERIOR NIGHT. VACARRO IN TREE. VOICE OF BABY DOLL AT PHONE.
BABY DOLL: I want the Police Chief. Yes, the Chief, not just the police, the Chief. This is Baby Doll McCorkle speaking, the ex-Mrs Meighan on Tiger Tail Road! My husband has got a shotgun and is threat'nin' to –
[*Her voice turns into a scream. She comes running out front door followed by* MEIGHAN. *She darts around side of house.* MEIGHAN *is very drunk now. He goes the opposite way around the house.* VACARRO *drops out of tree and gives* BABY DOLL *a low whistle. She rushes back to front yard.*]
BABY DOLL: Oh, Gah, Gah, watch out, he's got a shotgun. He's – crazy! I callt th' Chief of –
[VACARRO *leaps into tree again.*]
SILVA: Grab my hand! Quick! Now *up!* Up, now Baby Doll!
[*He hoists her into tree with him as the wild-eyed old bull comes charging back around house with his weapon. He blasts away at a shadow. (Yard is full of windy shadows.) He is sobbing.*]
ARCHIE: BABY DOLL! BABY! BABY! BABY DOLL! MY BABY.

[*Goes stumbling around back of house, great wind in the trees.*
BABY DOLL *rests in the arms of* VACARRO.
MEIGHAN *in back yard. Storm cellar door bangs open.*
MEIGHAN *fires through it. Then at chicken coop. Then into
wheelless limousine chassis in side yard, etc., etc.*
Shot of VACARRO *and* BABY DOLL *in fork of pecan tree.*]

SILVA: [*Grinning*] We're still playing hide-and-seek!

BABY DOLL: [*Excitedly, almost giggling*] How long you guess
we gonna be up this tree?

SILVA: I don't care. I'm *comfortable* – Are you?

[*Her answer is a sigh. He cracks a nut in his mouth and divides it
with her. She giggles and whispers, 'Shhhh!'*]

ARCHIE: [*Raving, sobbing, stumbling*] Baby, my baby, oh, Baby
Doll, my baby.... *Silence.* HEY! WOP! YELLOWBELLY!
WHERE ARE YUH?

[AUNT ROSE COMFORT *comes forlornly out on the porch,
weighed down by ancient suitcase, roped together.*]

AUNT ROSE: [*Fearfully, her hair blown wild by the wind*] Baby
Doll, honey? Honey? Baby Doll, honey?

ARCHIE: [*In back yard*] I SEE YOU! COME OUT OF THERE,
YOU YELLOWBELLY WOP, YOU!

[*Shotgun blasts away behind house.* AUNT ROSE COMFORT
*on front porch utters a low cry and drops her suitcase. Backs
against wall, hand to chest.*
Fade in police siren approaching down Tiger Tail Road.]

BABY DOLL: [*Nestling in* VACARRO'S *arms in tree*] I feel sorry
for poor old Aunt Rose Comfort. She doesn't know where
to go or what to do....

[*Moon comes briefly out and shines on their crouched figures in
fork on tree.*]

SILVA: [*Gently*] Does anyone know where to go, or what to
do?

114]

THE YARD. ANOTHER ANGLE. POLICE CAR
STOPPING BEFORE THE HOUSE AND MEN
JUMPING OUT.

[*Shot of* MEIGHAN *staggering and sobbing among the litter of uncollected garbage.*]

ARCHIE: Baby Doll, my baby! Yellow son of a —

115]

THE YARD. ANOTHER ANGLE. SHOT OF
AUNT ROSE COMFORT RETREATING INTO
SHADOW AS POLICE COME AROUND THE
HOUSE SUPPORTING ARCHIE LEE'S LIMP
FIGURE. SHOT OF COUPLE IN TREE AS
MOON GOES BACK OF CLOUDS.

[*Stillness. Dark.* AUNT ROSE COMFORT *begins to sing a hymn:* '*Rock of Ages*'.]

AUNT ROSE: Rock of ages, cleft for me,
   Let me hide myself in Thee!

[VACARRO *drops out of tree and stands with arms lifted for* BABY DOLL.]

SOMETHING UNSPOKEN

To
Anne Meacham

SOMETHING UNSPOKEN

[MISS CORNELIA SCOTT, 60, *a wealthy Southern spinster, is seated at a small mahogany table which is set for two. The other place, not yet occupied, has a single rose in a crystal vase before it.* MISS SCOTT's *position at the table is flanked by a cradle phone, a silver tray of mail, and an ornate silver coffee urn. An imperial touch is given by purple velvet drapes directly behind her figure at the table. A console phonograph is at edge of lighted area.*
At rise she is dialling a number on the phone.]

CORNELIA: Is this Mrs Horton Reid's residence? I am calling for Miss Cornelia Scott. Miss Scott is sorry that she will not be able to attend the meeting of the Confederate Daughters this afternoon as she woke up this morning with a sore throat and has to remain in bed, and will you kindly give her apologies to Mrs Reid for not letting her know sooner. Thank you. Oh, wait a moment! I think Miss Scott has another message.

[GRACE LANCASTER *enters the lighted area.* CORNELIA *raises her hand in a warning gesture.*]

– What is it, Miss Scott?

[*Brief pause.*]

Oh. Miss Scott would like to leave word for Miss Esmeralda Hawkins to call her as soon as she arrives. Thank you. Goodbye. [*Hangs up.*] You see I am having to impersonate my secretary this morning!

GRACE: The light was so dim it didn't wake me up.

[*Grace Lancaster is 40 or 45, faded, but still pretty. Her blonde hair, greying slightly, her pale eyes, her thin figure, in a pink silk dressing-gown, give her an insubstantial quality in sharp contrast to Miss Scott's Roman grandeur. There is between the two women a mysterious tension, an atmosphere of something unspoken.*]

95

CORNELIA: I've already opened the mail.

GRACE: Anything of interest?

CORNELIA: A card from Thelma Peterson at Mayo's.

GRACE: Oh, how is Thelma?

CORNELIA: She says she's 'progressing nicely' whatever that indicates.

GRACE: Didn't she have something removed?

CORNELIA: Several things, I believe.

GRACE: Oh, here's the Fortnightly Review of Current Letters!

CORNELIA: Much to my astonishment. I thought I had cancelled my subscription to that publication.

GRACE: Really, Cornelia?

CORNELIA: Surely you remember. I cancelled my subscription immediately after the issue came out with that scurrilous attack on my cousin, Cecil Tutwiler Bates, the only dignified novelist the South has produced since Thomas Nelson Page.

GRACE: Oh, yes, I do remember. You wrote a furious letter of protest to the editor of the magazine and you received such a conciliatory reply from an associate editor named Caroline Something or Other that you were completely mollified and cancelled the cancellation!

CORNELIA: I have never been mollified by conciliatory replies, never completely and never even partially, and if I wrote to the editor in chief and was answered by an associate editor, my reaction to that piece of impertinence would hardly be what you call 'mollified'.

GRACE [to change the subject]: Oh, here's the new catalogue from the Gramophone Shoppe in Atlanta!

CORNELIA [conceding a point]: Yes, there it is.

GRACE: I see you've checked several items.

CORNELIA: I think we ought to build up our collection of Lieder.

GRACE: You've checked a Sibelius that we already have.

CORNELIA: It's getting a little bit scratchy. [Inhales deeply and sighs, her look fastened upon the silent phone.] – You'll also notice that I've checked a few operatic selections.

GRACE [*excitedly*]: Where, which ones, I don't see them!

CORNELIA: – Why are you so excited over the catalogue, dear?

GRACE: I adore phonograph records!

CORNELIA: I wish you adored them enough to put them back in their proper places in albums.

GRACE: Oh, here's the Vivaldi we wanted!

CORNELIA: Not 'we' dear. Just you.

GRACE: Not *you*, Cornelia?

CORNELIA: I think Vivaldi's a very thin shadow of Bach.

GRACE: – How strange that I should have the impression you –

    [*Phone rings.*]

    – Shall I answer?

CORNELIA: If you will be so kind.

GRACE [*lifting receiver*]: *Miss Scott's* residence! [*This announcement is made in a tone of reverence, as though mentioning a seat of holiness.*] Oh, no, this is Grace, but Cornelia is right by my side. [*Passing phone*] Esmeralda Hawkins.

CORNELIA [*grimly*]: I've been expecting her call. [*Into phone*] Hello, Esmeralda, my dear. I've been expecting your call. Now where are you calling me from? Of course I know that you're calling me from the meeting, *ça va sans dire, ma petite!* Ha ha! But from which phone in the house; there's two, you know, the one in the downstairs hall and the one in the chatelaine's boudoir where the ladies will probably be removing their wraps. Oh. You're on the downstairs', are you? Well, by this time I presume that practically all the Daughters have assembled. Now go upstairs and call me back from there so we can talk with a little more privacy, dear, as I want to make my position very clear before the meeting commences. Thank you dear. [*Hangs up. Looks grimly into space.*]

GRACE: – The – Confederate Daughters?

CORNELIA: Yes! They're holding the Annual Election today.

GRACE: Oh, how exciting! Why aren't you at the meeting?

CORNELIA: I preferred not to go.

GRACE: You preferred *not* to go?

CORNELIA: Yes, I preferred not to go.... [*She touches her chest, breathing heavily as if she had run upstairs.*]

GRACE: But it's the annual election of officers!

CORNELIA: Yes! I told you it was!

[GRACE *drops spoon.* CORNELIA *cries out and jumps a little.*]

GRACE: I'm so sorry! [*Rings bell for servant.*]

CORNELIA: Intrigue, intrigue and duplicity, revolt me so that I wouldn't be able to breathe in the same atmosphere!

[GRACE *rings bell louder.*]

Why are you ringing that bell? You know Lucinda's not here!

GRACE: I'm so sorry. Where has Lucinda gone?

CORNELIA [*in a hoarse whisper, barely audible*]: There's a big coloured funeral in town. [*Clears throat violently and repeats the statement.*]

GRACE: Oh, dear. You have that nervous laryngitis.

CORNELIA: No sleep, no sleep last night.

[*Phone screams at her elbow. She cries out and thrusts it from her as if it were on fire.*]

GRACE [*lifting phone*]: Miss Scott's residence. Oh. Just a moment please.

CORNELIA [*snatching phone*]: *Esmeralda, are you upstairs now?*

GRACE [*in a loud whisper*]: It isn't Esmeralda. It's Mrs C. C. Bright!

CORNELIA: One moment, one moment, one moment! [*Thrusts phone back at Grace with a glare of fury.*] How dare you put me on the line with that woman!

GRACE: Cornelia, I didn't, I was just going to ask if you –

CORNELIA: Hush! [*She springs back from table, glaring across it.*] – Now give me that phone. [GRACE *hands it to her. Coldly*] What can I do for you, please? No. I'm afraid that my garden will not be open to the Pilgrims this spring. I think the cultivation of gardens is an aesthetic hobby and not a competitive sport. Individual visitors will be welcome if they call in advance so that I can arrange for my gardener to show them around, but no bands of Pilgrims, not after the devastation my garden suffered last spring – Pilgrims coming with dogs – picking flowers and – You're entirely welcome, yes, goodbye! [*Returns phone to Grace.*]

GRACE: I think the election would have been less of a strain if you'd gone to it, Cornelia.

CORNELIA: I don't know what you are talking about.

GRACE: Aren't you up for office?

CORNELIA: 'Up for office?' What is 'up for office'?

GRACE: Why, ha ha! – *running* for – something?

CORNELIA: – Have you ever known me to '*run*' for anything, Grace? Whenever I've held an office in a society or club it's been at the *insistence* of the members, because I really have an *aversion* to holding office. But this is a different thing, a different thing altogether. It's a test of something. You see, I have known for some time, now, that there is a little group, a *clique*, in the Daughters which is hostile to me!

GRACE: Oh, Cornelia, I'm sure you must be mistaken.

CORNELIA: No. There is a movement against me.

GRACE: A movement? A movement against you?

CORNELIA: An organized movement to keep me out of any important office.

GRACE: But haven't you always held some important office in the Chapter?

CORNELIA: I have never been *Regent* of it!

GRACE: Oh, you want to be *Regent*?

CORNELIA: No. You misunderstand me. I don't '*want*' to be Regent.

GRACE: Oh?

CORNELIA: I don't 'want' to be anything whatsoever. I simply want to break up this movement against me, and for that purpose I have rallied my forces.

GRACE: – Your – *forces*? [*Her lips twitch slightly as if she had a hysterical impulse to smile.*]

CORNELIA: Yes. I still have some friends in the Chapter who have resisted the movement.

GRACE: Oh?

CORNELIA: I have the solid support of all the older Board members.

GRACE: Why, then, I should think you'd have nothing to worry about!

CORNELIA: The Chapter has expanded too rapidly lately. Women have been admitted that couldn't get into a front pew at the Second Baptist Church! And that's the disgraceful truth. . . .

GRACE: – But since it's really a patriotic society . . .

CORNELIA: My dear Grace, there are two chapters of the Confederate Daughters in the city of Meridian. There is the Forrest Chapter, which is for social riff-raff, and there is *this* Chapter which was *supposed* to have a *little* bit of *distinction*! I'm not a snob. I'm nothing if not democratic. You know *that*! But –

[*Phone rings.* CORNELIA *reaches for it. Then pushes it to Grace.*]

GRACE: Miss Scott's residence! Oh, yes, yes, just a moment! [*Passes phone to Cornelia.*] It's Esmeralda Hawkins.

CORNELIA [*into phone*]: Are you upstairs now, dear? Well, I wondered. It took you so long to call back. Oh, but I thought you said the luncheon was over. Well, I'm glad that you fortified yourself with a bite to eat. What did the buffet consist of? Chicken *à la king*! Wouldn't you know it! That is so characteristic of poor Amelia! With bits of pimento and tiny mushrooms in it? What did the ladies counting their calories do! Nibbled around the edges? Oh, poor dears! – and afterwards I suppose there was lemon sherbet with lady-fingers? What, lime sherbet! And *no* lady-fingers? *What a departure!* What a *shocking* apostasy! I'm quite stunned! Ho ho ho . . . [*Reaches shakily for cup.*] – Now what's going on? Discussing the Civil Rights Programme? Then they won't take the vote for at least half an hour! – Now, Esmeralda, I *do* hope that you understand my position clearly. I don't wish to hold any office in the Chapter unless it's by acclamation. You know what that means, don't you? It's a parliamentary term. It means when someone is desired for an office so unanimously that no vote has to be taken. In other words, elected automatically, simply by nomination, unopposed. Yes, my dear; it's just as simple as that. I have served as Treasurer for three terms, twice as Secretary, once as Chaplain – and what a dreary office that was with those long-drawn prayers for the Confederate dead! – Altogether I've served on the Board for, let's see, fourteen years! – Well, now, my dear, the point is simply this, If the Daughters feel that I have demonstrated my capabilities and loyalty strongly enough that I should simply be named as Regent without a vote being taken – by unanimous acclamation! – why, then, of course I would feel obliged to accept.... [*Her voice trembles with emotion.*] – But if, on the other hand, the – uh – *clique*! – and you know the ones I mean! – is bold enough to propose someone else for the office – Do you understand my position? In that eventuality, hard as it is to imagine, – I prefer to bow out of the picture entirely! – The moment another nomination is made and seconded, my own must be withdrawn, at once, unconditionally! Is that quite understood, Esmeralda? Then good! Go back downstairs to the meeting. Digest your chicken *à la king*, my dear, and call me again on the upstairs phone as soon as there's something to tell me.

[*Hangs up and stares grimly into space.* GRACE *lifts a section of grapefruit on a tiny silver fork.*]

GRACE: They haven't had it yet?

CORNELIA: Had what, dear?

GRACE: The election!

CORNELIA: No, not yet. It seems to be – imminent, though.
. . .

GRACE: Cornelia, why don't you think about something else until it's over!

CORNELIA: What makes you think that I am nervous about it?

GRACE: You're – you're *breathing* so fast!

CORNELIA: I didn't sleep well last night. You were prowling about the house with that stitch in your side.

GRACE: I *am* so sorry. You know it's nothing. A muscular contraction that comes from strain.

CORNELIA: What strain does it come from, Grace?

GRACE: What strain? [*Utters a faint, perplexed laugh.*] Why! – I don't know....

CORNELIA: The strain of *what*? Would you like *me* to tell you?

GRACE: – Excuse me, I – [*Rises.*]

CORNELIA [*sharply*]: Where are you going?

GRACE: Upstairs for a moment! I just remembered I should have taken my drops of belladonna!

CORNELIA: It does no good *after* eating.

GRACE: I suppose that's right. It doesn't.

CORNELIA: But you want to escape?

GRACE: Of course not. . . .

CORNELIA: Several times lately you've rushed away from me as if I'd suddenly threatened you with a knife.

GRACE: Cornelia! – I've been – jumpy!

CORNELIA: It's always when something is almost – *spoken* – between us!

GRACE: – I hate to see you so agitated over the outcome of a silly club-woman's election!

CORNELIA: I'm not talking about the Daughters. I'm not even thinking about them, I'm –

GRACE: I wish you'd dismiss it completely from your mind. Now would be a good time to play some records. Let me put a symphony on the machine!

CORNELIA: No.

GRACE: How about the Bach for piano and strings! The one we received for Christmas from Jessie and Gay?

CORNELIA: No, I said, No, I said, No!

GRACE: – Something very light and quiet, then! The old French madrigals, maybe?

CORNELIA: Anything to avoid a talk between us? Anything to evade a conversation, especially when the servant is not in the house?

GRACE: Oh, here it is! This is just the thing! [*She has started the phonograph. Landowska playing a harpsichord selection. The phonograph is at the edge of the lighted area or just outside it.* CORNELIA *stares grimly as* GRACE *resumes her seat with an affection of enchantment, clasping her hands and closing her eyes. Enchanted*] Oh, how it smooths things over, how sweet, and gentle, and – pure. . . .

CORNELIA: – Yes! And completely dishonest!

GRACE: Music? Dishonest?

CORNELIA: Completely! It 'smooths things over' instead of –
speaking them out . . .

GRACE: 'Music hath charms to soothe the savage breast.'

CORNELIA: Yes, oh, yes. If the savage breast permits it.

GRACE: Oh, sublime – sublime. . . .

CORNELIA [*grudgingly*]: Landowska is an artist of rare pre-
cision.

GRACE [*ecstatically*]: And such a noble face, a profile as fine
and strong as Edith Sitwell's. After this we'll play Edith
Sitwell's *Façade*. 'Jane, Jane, tall as a crane, the morning
light creaks down again. . . .'

CORNELIA: Dearest, isn't there something you've failed to
notice?

GRACE: – Where?

CORNELIA: Right under your nose.

GRACE: Oh! You mean my flower?

CORNELIA: Yes! I mean your rose!

GRACE: Of course I noticed my rose. The moment I came in
the room I saw it here!

CORNELIA: You made no allusion to it.

GRACE: I would have, but you were so concerned over the
meeting.

CORNELIA: I'm not concerned over the meeting.

GRACE: – Whom do I have to thank for this lovely rose? My
gracious employer?

CORNELIA: You will find fourteen others on your desk in the
library when you go in to take care of the correspondence.

GRACE: Fourteen other roses?

CORNELIA: A total of fifteen!

GRACE: How wonderful! – Why fifteen?

CORNELIA: How long have you been here, dearest? How
long have you made this house a house of roses?

GRACE: – What a nice way to put it! Why, of course! I've
been your secretary for fifteen years!

CORNELIA: Fifteen years my companion! A rose for every
year, a year for every rose!

GRACE: What a charming sort of a way to – observe the –
occasion. . . .

CORNELIA: First I thought 'Pearls' and then I thought; No, roses. But perhaps I should have given you something golden, ha ha! – Silence is golden, they say!

GRACE: Oh, dear, that stupid machine is playing the same record over!

CORNELIA: Let it, let it, I like it!

GRACE: Just let me –

CORNELIA: Sit down!! – It was fifteen years ago this very morning, on the sixth day of November, that someone very sweet and gentle and silent! – a shy, little, quiet little widow! – arrived for the first time at Seven Edgewater Drive. The season was autumn. I had been raking dead leaves over the rose-bushes to protect them from frost when I heard footsteps on the gravel – light, quick, delicate footsteps like spring coming in the middle of autumn – and looked up, and sure enough, there spring was! A little person so thin that light shone through her as if she were made of the silk of a white parasol!

[GRACE *utters a short, startled laugh.*]

[*Harshly; wounded*] – Why did you laugh? Why did you laugh like that?

GRACE: It sounded – ha ha! – it sounded like the first paragraph of a woman's magazine story.

CORNELIA: – What a cutting remark!

GRACE: I didn't mean it that way, I –

CORNELIA: What other way could you mean it!

GRACE: Cornelia, you know how I am! I'm always a little embarrassed by sentiment, aren't I?

CORNELIA: Yes. Frightened of anything that betrays some feeling!

GRACE: People who don't know you well, nearly all people we know, would be astounded to hear you, Cornelia Scott, that grave and dignified lady, expressing herself in such a lyrical manner!

CORNELIA: People who don't know me well are everybody! Yes, I think even *you*!

GRACE: Cornelia, you must admit that sentiment isn't like you!

CORNELIA: *Is nothing like me but silence?*
[*Clock ticks loudly.*]
Am I sentenced to silence for a lifetime?

GRACE: – It's just not like you to –

CORNELIA: Not like me. Not like me. What do you know what's like me or not like me!

GRACE: You may deny it, Cornelia, as much as you please, but it's evident to me that you are completely unstrung by your anxieties over the Confederate Daughters' election!

CORNELIA: – Another thinly veiled insult?

GRACE: Oh, Cornelia, please!

CORNELIA [*imitating her gesture*]: 'Oh, Cornelia, please!!'

GRACE: If I've said anything wrong, I beg your pardon, I offer my very humble apologies for it.

CORNELIA: I don't want apologies from you.
[*Strained silence. Clock ticks. Suddenly* GRACE *reaches across to touch the veined jewelled hand of Miss Scott.* CORNELIA *snatches her own hand away as though the touch had burned her.*]

GRACE: Thank you for the roses.

CORNELIA: I don't want thanks from you either. All that I want is a little return of affection – not much, but sometimes a little!

GRACE: You have that always, Cornelia.

CORNELIA: And one thing more: a little outspokenness, too.

GRACE: – Outspokenness?

CORNELIA: Yes, outspokenness, if that's not too much to ask from such a proud young lady!

GRACE [*rising from table*]: I am not proud and I am not young, Cornelia.

CORNELIA: Sit down. Don't leave the table.

GRACE: Is that an order?

CORNELIA: I don't give orders to you, I make requests!

GRACE: Sometimes the requests of an employer are hard to distinguish from orders. [*She sits down.*]

CORNELIA: Please turn off the victrola.
[GRACE *rises and stops the machine.*]
Grace! – Don't you feel there's – *something unspoken* between
?

GRACE: No. No, I don't.

CORNELIA: I do. I've felt for a long time something unspoken between us.

GRACE: – Don't you think there is always something unspoken between two people?

CORNELIA: I see no reason for it.

GRACE: But don't a great many things exist without reason?

CORNELIA: Let's not turn this into a metaphysical discussion.

GRACE: All right. But you mystify me.

CORNELIA: It's very simple. It's just that I feel that there's something unspoken between us that ought to be spoken. – – Why are you looking at me like that?

GRACE: How am I looking at you?

CORNELIA: With positive terror!

GRACE: Cornelia!

CORNELIA: You are, you are, but I'm not going to be shut up!

GRACE: Go on, continue, please, do!

CORNELIA: I'm going to, I will, I will, I –

[*Phone rings.* GRACE *reaches for it.*]

No, no, no, let it ring!

[*It goes on ringing.*]

Take it off the hook!

GRACE: Do just let me –

CORNELIA: Off the hook I told you!

[GRACE *takes phone off hook. A voice says; 'Hello? Hello? Hello? Hello?'*]

GRACE [*suddenly sobbing*]: I can't stand it!

CORNELIA: *Be* STILL! *Someone can hear you!*

Voice: Hello? Hello? Cornelia? Cornelia Scott?

[CORNELIA *seizes phone and slams it back into cradle.*]

CORNELIA: Now stop that! Stop that silly little female trick!

GRACE: You say there's something unspoken. Maybe there is. I don't know. But I do know some things are better left unspoken. Also I know that when a silence between two people has gone on for a long time it's like a wall that's impenetrable between them! Maybe between us there is such a wall. One that's impenetrable. Or maybe *you* can break it. I know I can't. I can't even attempt to. You're the strong one of us two, and surely you know it. - Both of us have turned grey! - But not the same kind of grey. In that velvet dressing-gown you look like the Emperor Tiberius! - In his imperial toga! - Your hair and your eyes are both the colour of iron! Iron-grey. Invincible-looking! People are nearly all somewhat - frightened of you. They feel your force and they admire you for it. They come to you here for opinions on this or that. What plays are good on Broadway this season, what books are worth reading and what books are trash and what - what records are valuable and - what is the proper attitude toward - Bills in Congress! - Oh, you're a fountain of wisdom! - And in addition to that, you have your - *wealth*! Yes, you have your - *fortune*! - All of your real-estate holdings, your blue-chip stocks, your - bonds, your - mansion on Edgewater Drive, your - shy little - secretary, your - fabulous gardens that Pilgrims cannot go into. . . .

CORNELIA: Oh, yes, now you are speaking, now you are speaking at last! Go on, please go on speaking.

GRACE: I am - very - different! - Also turning grey, but my grey is different. Not iron, like yours, not imperial, Cornelia, but grey, yes, grey, the - colour of a - *cobweb*. . . . [*She starts the record again, very softly.*] - Something white getting soiled, the grey of something forgotten.

[*Phone rings again. Neither of them seems to notice it.*]
- And that being the case, that being the difference between our two kinds of grey, yours and mine - You mustn't expect me to give bold answers to questions that make the house shake with silence! To speak out things that are fifteen years unspoken!? - That long a time can make a silence a wall that nothing less than dynamite could break through and - [*Picks up phone*] I'm not strong enough, bold enough, I'm not -

CORNELIA [*fiercely*]: You're speaking into the phone!

GRACE [*into phone*]: Hello? Oh, yes, she's here. It's Esmeralda Hawkins.

CORNELIA [*snatches the phone*]: What is it, Esmeralda? What are you saying? Is the room full of women? Such a babble of voices! What are you trying to tell me? Have they held the election already? What, what, what? Oh, this is maddening! I can't hear a word that you're saying. It sounds like the Fourth of July, a great celebration! Ha ha! Now try once more with your mouth closer to the phone! What, what? Would I be willing to what? You can't be serious! Are you out of your mind? [*To Grace in a panicky voice*] She wants to know if I would be willing to serve as *Vice*-Regent! [*Back into phone*] Esmeralda! Will you listen to me? What's going on! Are there some fresh defections? How does it look? Why did you call me again before the vote? Louder, please speak louder, and cup your mouth to the phone in case they're eavesdropping! Who asked if I would accept the Vice-Regency, dear? Oh, Mrs Colby, of course! – that treacherous witch! – *Esmeralda!* Listen! I – WILL ACCEPT – NO OFFICE – EXCEPT – THE HIGHEST! Did you understand that? I – WILL ACCEPT NO OFFICE EXCEPT – ESMERALDA! [*Drops phone into cradle.*]

GRACE: – Have they held the election?

CORNELIA [*dazed*]: What? – No, there's a five-minute recess before the election begins. . . .

GRACE: – Things are not going well?

CORNELIA: 'Would you accept the Vice-Regency' she asked me, 'if for some reason they don't elect you Regent?' – Then she hung up as if somebody had snatched the phone away from her, or the house had – caught fire!

GRACE: You shouted so I think she must have been frightened.

CORNELIA: – Whom can you trust in this world, whom can you ever rely on?

GRACE: I think perhaps you should have gone to the meeting.

CORNELIA: I think my not being there is much more pointed.

GRACE [*rising again*]: May I be excused, now?

CORNELIA: No! Stay here!

GRACE: If that is just a request, I –

CORNELIA: That's an order!

[GRACE *sits down and closes her eyes.*]

CORNELIA: When you first came to this house – do you know I didn't expect you?

GRACE: Oh, but, Cornelia, you'd invited me here.

CORNELIA: We hardly knew each other.

GRACE: We'd met the summer before, when Ralph was –

CORNELIA: – Living! Yes, we met at Sewanee, where he was a summer instructor.

GRACE: – He was already ill.

CORNELIA: I thought what a pity that lovely, delicate girl hasn't found someone she could lean on, who could protect her! And two months later I heard through Clarabelle Drake that he was dead. . . .

GRACE: You wrote me such a sweet letter, saying how lonely you were since the loss of your mother and urging me to rest here till the shock was over. You seemed to understand how badly I needed to withdraw for a while from – old associations. I hesitated to come. I didn't until you wrote me a second letter. . . .

CORNELIA: – After I received yours. You wanted urging.

GRACE: I wanted to be quite sure I was really wanted! I only came intending to stay a few weeks. I was so afraid that I would outstay my welcome!

CORNELIA: How blind of you not to see how desperately I wanted to keep you here for ever!

GRACE: Oh, I did see that you –

[*Phone rings. She snatches it up.*]

Miss Scott's residence! – Yes, she's here.

CORNELIA [*snatches it finally up*]: – Cornelia Scott speaking! Oh. It's you, Esmeralda! Well, how did it come out? – *I don't believe you! I simply don't believe you.* . . .

[GRACE *sits down quietly at the table.*]

– MRS HORNSBY ELECTED? Well, there's a dark horse for you! Less than a year in the Chapter. . . . Did you – nominate me? – Oh – I see! But I told you to withdraw my name if – No, no, no, don't explain, it doesn't matter, I have too much already. You know I am going into the Daughters of the Barons of Runnymede! Yes; it's been established, I have a direct line to the Earl of – No, it's been straightened out, a clear line is established, and then, of course, I am also eligible for the Colonial Dames and for the Huguenot Society, and what with all my other activities and so forth, why, I couldn't *possibly* have taken it on if they'd – *wanted* ... Of course I'm going to resign from the local Chapter! Oh, yes, I am! My secretary is sitting right here by me. She has her pencil, her notebook! I'm going to dictate my letter of resignation from the local Chapter the moment that I hang up on this conversation. Oh, no, no, no, I'm not mad, not outraged, at all. I'm just a little – ha ha! – a little – amused. ... MRS HORNSBY? Nothing succeeds like mediocrity, does it?! Thanks and goodbye, Esmeralda.

[*Hangs up; stunned.* GRACE *rises.*]

GRACE: Notebook and pencil?

CORNELIA: Yes. Notebook and pencil.... – I have to – dictate a letter ...

[GRACE *leaves the table. Just at the edge of the lighted area, she turns to glance at Cornelia's rigid shoulders, and a slight, equivocal smile appears momentarily on her face; not quite malicious, but not really sympathetic. Then she crosses out of the light. A moment later her voice comes from the outer dark.*]

GRACE: *What lovely roses! One for every year!*

CURTAIN

SUMMER AND SMOKE

Who, if I were to cry out, would hear me among the angelic orders?

RILKE

SCENES

The entire action of the play takes place in Glorious Hill, Mississippi. The time is the turn of the century through 1916.

THE CAST

The first London production of this play was at the Lyric Theatre, Hammersmith, on Thursday, 22 November 1951, with the following cast:

ALMA WINEMILLER	*Margaret Johnston*
JOHN BUCHANAN	*William Sylvester*
MRS WINEMILLER	*Megs Jenkins*
REV. WINEMILLER	*Allan Jeayes*
PEARL	*Barbara Graley*
DUSTY	*Gaylord Cavallaro*
DR BUCHANAN	*Wensley Pithey*
ROSA GONZALES	*Ingeborg Wells*
NELLIE EWELL	*Sheila Shand Gibbs*
ROGER DOREMUS	*Peter Sallis*
MRS BASSETT	*Joan Young*
VERNON	*Sheldon Allan*
ROSEMARY	*Maria Britnieva*
PAPA GONZALES	*Reginald Dyson*
MR KRAMER	*Harry Towb*

Directed by PETER GLENVILLE

Décor by REECE PEMBERTON

Costumes by WILLIAM CHAPPELL

Original Music composed by PAUL BOWLES

AUTHOR'S PRODUCTION NOTES

As the concept of a design grows out of reading a play I will not do more than indicate what I think are the most essential points.

First of all – *The Sky*.

There must be a great expanse of sky so that the entire action of the play takes place against it. This is true of interior as well as exterior scenes. But in fact there are no really interior scenes, for the walls are omitted or just barely suggested by certain necessary fragments such as might be needed to hang a picture or to contain a door-frame.

During the day scenes the sky should be a pure and intense blue (like the sky of Italy as it is so faithfully represented in the religous paintings of the Renaissance) and costumes should be selected to form a dramatic colour contrast to this intense blue which the figures stand against. (Colour harmonies and other visual effects are tremendously important.)

In the night scenes, the more familiar constellations, such as Orion and the Great Bear and the Pleiades, are clearly projected on the night sky, and above them, splashed across the top of the cyclorama, is the nebulous radiance of the Milky Way. Fleecy cloud forms may also be projected on this cyclorama and made to drift across it.

So much for *The Sky*.

Now we descend to the so-called interior sets of the play. There are two of these 'interior' sets, one being the parlour of an episcopal rectory and the other the home of a doctor next door to the rectory. The architecture of these houses is barely suggested but is of an American Gothic design of the Victorian era. There are no actual doors or windows or walls. Doors and windows are represented by delicate framework of Gothic design. These frames have strings of ivy clinging to them, the leaves of emerald and amber. Sections of wall are used only where they are functionally required. There should be a fragment of wall in back of the rectory sofa, supporting a romantic landscape in a gilt frame. In the doctor's house there should be a section of a wall to support the chart of anatomy. Chirico has used fragmentary walls and interiors in a very evocative way in his painting called *Conversation among the Ruins*. We will deal more specifically with these interiors as we come to them in the course of the play.

Now we come to the main exterior set which is a promontory in a park or public square in the town of Glorious Hill. Situated on this promontory is a fountain in the form of a stone angel, in a gracefully crouching position with wings lifted and her hands held together to form a cup from which water flows, a public drinking fountain. The stone angel of the fountain should probably be elevated so that it appears in the background of the interior scenes as a symbolic figure (Eternity) brooding over the course of the play. *This entire exterior set may be on an upper level, above that of the two fragmentary interiors.* I would like all three units to form an harmonious whole like one complete picture rather than three separate ones. An imaginative designer may solve these plastic problems in a variety of ways and should not feel bound by any of my specific suggestions.

There is one more set, a very small exterior representing an arbour, which we will describe when we reach it.

Everything possible should be done to give an unbroken fluid quality to the sequence of scenes.

There should be no curtain except for the intermission. The other divisions of the play should be accomplished by changes of lighting.

Finally, the matter of music. One basic theme should recur and the points of recurrence have been indicated here and there in the stage directions.

Rome, March 1948

PROLOGUE

————◆◆◆————

In the park near the angel of the fountain. At dusk of an evening in May, in the first few years of this century.

ALMA, *as a child of ten, comes into the scene. She wears a middy blouse and has ribboned braids. She already has the dignity of an adult; there is a quality of extraordinary delicacy and tenderness or spirituality in her, which must set her distinctly apart from other children. She has a habit of holding her hands, one cupped under the other in a way similar to that of receiving the wafer at Holy Communion. This is a habit that will remain with her as an adult. She stands like that in front of the stone angel for a few moments; then bends to drink at the fountain.*

While she is bent at the fountain, JOHN, *as a child, enters. He shoots a pea-shooter at* ALMA's *bent-over back. She utters a startled cry and whirls about. He laughs.*

JOHN: Hi, preacher's daughter. [*He advances towards her.*] I been looking for you.

ALMA [*hopefully*]: You have?

JOHN: Was it you that put them handkerchiefs on my desk?

    [ALMA *smiles uncertainly.*]

  Answer up!

ALMA: I put a box of handkerchiefs on your desk.

JOHN: I figured it was you. What was the idea, Miss Priss?

ALMA: You needed them.

JOHN: Trying to make a fool of me?

ALMA: Oh, no!

JOHN: Then what was the idea?

ALMA: You have a bad cold and your nose has been running all week. It spoils your appearance.

JOHN: You don't have to look at me if you don't like my appearance.

ALMA: I like your appearance.

JOHN [*coming closer*]: Is that why you look at me all the time?

ALMA: I – don't!

JOHN: Oh, yeh, you do. You been keeping your eyes on me all the time. Every time I look around I see them cat eyes of yours looking at me. That was the trouble today when Miss Blanchard asked you where the River Amazon was. She asked you twice and you still didn't answer because you w' lookin' at me. What's the idea? What've y' got on y' mind anyhow? Answer up!

ALMA: I was only thinking how handsome you'd be if your face wasn't dirty. You know why your face is dirty? Because you don't use a handkerchief and you wipe your nose on the sleeve of that dirty old sweater.

JOHN [*indignantly*]: Hah!

ALMA: That's why I put the handkerchiefs on your desk and I wrapped them up so nobody would know what they were. It isn't my fault that you opened the box in front of everybody!

JOHN: What did you think I'd do with a strange box on my desk? Just leave it there till it exploded or something? Sure I opened it up. I didn't expect to find no – *handkerchiefs!* – in it ...

ALMA [*in a shy trembling voice*]: I'm sorry that you were embarrassed. I honestly am awfully sorry that you were embarrassed. Because I wouldn't embarrass you for the world!

JOHN: Don't flatter yourself that I was embarrassed. I don't embarrass that easy.

ALMA: It was stupid and cruel of those girls to laugh.

JOHN: Hah!

ALMA: They should all realize that you don't have a mother to take care of such things for you. It was a pleasure to me to be able to do something for you, only I didn't want you to know it was me who did it.

JOHN: Hee-haw! Ho-hum! Take 'em back! [*He snatches out the box and thrusts it towards her.*]

ALMA: *Please* keep them.

JOHN: What do I want with them?

[ALMA *stares at* JOHN *helplessly. He tosses the box to the ground and goes up to the fountain and drinks. Something in her face mollifies him and he sits down at the base of the fountain with a manner that does not preclude a more friendly relation. The dusk gathers deeper.*]

JOHN: Does she have a name?

ALMA: Yes, I found out she does. It's carved in the base, but its' all worn away so you can't make it out with your eyes.

JOHN: Then how do you know it?

ALMA: You have to read it with your fingers. I did and it gave me cold shivers! *You* read it and see if it doesn't give *you* cold shivers. Go on! Read it with your fingers!

JOHN: Why don't you tell me and save the trouble?

ALMA: I'm not going to tell you.

[JOHN *grins indulgently and turns to the pediment, crouching before it and running his fingers along the worn inscription.*]

JOHN: E?

ALMA: Yes, E is the first letter!

JOHN: T?

ALMA: Yes!

JOHN: E?

ALMA: E!

JOHN: K?

ALMA: No, no, not K! – R!

[*He slowly straightens up.*]

JOHN: Eternity?

ALMA: *Eternity!* – Didn't it give you the cold shivers?

JOHN: Nahh.

ALMA: Well, it did me!

JOHN: Because you're a preacher's daughter. Eternity. What is eternity?

ALMA [*in a hushed wondering voice*]: It's something that goes on and on when life and death and time and everything else is all through with.

JOHN: There's no such thing.

ALMA: There is. It's what people's souls live in when they have left their bodies. My name is Alma and Alma is Spanish for soul. Did you know that?

JOHN: Hee-haw! Ho-hum! Have you ever seen a dead person?

ALMA: No.

JOHN: I have. They made me go in the room when my mother was dying and she caught hold of my hand and wouldn't let me go – and so I screamed and hit her.

ALMA: Oh, you didn't do that.

JOHN [*sombrely*]: Uh-huh. She didn't look like my mother. Her face was all ugly and yellow and – terrible – bad-smelling! And so I hit her to make her let go of my hand. They told me that I was a devil!

ALMA: You didn't know what you were doing.

JOHN: My dad is a doctor.

ALMA: I know.

JOHN: He wants to send me to college to study to be a doctor but I wouldn't be a doctor for the world. And have to go in a room and watch people dying! . . . Jesus.

ALMA: You'll change your mind about that.

JOHN: Oh, no, I won't. I'd rather *be* a devil, like they called me and go to South America on a boat! . . . Give me one of them handkerchiefs.

[ALMA *brings them eagerly and humbly to the fountain.* JOHN *takes one out and wets it at the fountain and scrubs his face with it.*]

Is my face clean enough to suit you now?

ALMA: Yes! – Beautiful!

JOHN: *What!*

ALMA: I said 'Beautiful'!

JOHN: Well – let's – kiss each other.

ALMA *turns away.*]

Come on, let's just try it!

[JOHN *seizes her shoulders and gives her a quick rough kiss. She stands amazed, with one hand cupping the other.*

The voice of a child in the distance calls: '*Johnny! Johnny!*'

JOHN *suddenly snatches at* ALMA'*s hair-ribbon, jerks it loose and then runs off with a mocking laugh.*

Hurt and bewildered, ALMA *turns back to the stone angel, for comfort. She crouches at the pediment and touches the inscription with her fingers. The scene dims out with music.*]

PART ONE: A SUMMER

❦

SCENE I

Before the curtain rises a band is heard playing a patriotic anthem, punctuated with the crackle of fireworks.

The scene is the same as for the Prologue. It is the evening of 4 July in a year shortly before the First World War. There is a band concert and a display of fireworks in the park. During the scene the light changes from faded sunlight to dusk. Sections of roof, steeples, weather-vanes, should have a metallic surface that catches the mellow light on the back-drop; when dusk has fallen the stars should be visible.

As the curtain rises, the REV. *and* MRS WINEMILLER *come in and sit on the bench near the fountain.*

MRS WINEMILLER *was a spoiled and selfish girl who evaded responsibilities of later life by slipping into a state of perverse childishness. She is known as* MR WINEMILLER*'s 'Cross'.*

MR WINEMILLER [*suddenly rising*]: There is Alma, getting on the bandstand!

    [MRS WINEMILLER *is dreamily munching popcorn.*]

AN ANNOUNCER'S VOICE [*at a distance*]: The Glorious Hill Orchestra brings you Miss Alma Winemiller, The Nightingale of the Delta, singing . . . 'La Golondrina'.

MR WINEMILLER [*sitting back down again*]: This is going to provoke a lot of criticism.

    [*The song commences. The voice is not particularly strong, but it has great purity and emotion.* JOHN BUCHANAN *comes along. He is now a Promethean figure, brilliantly and restlessly alive in a stagnant society. The excess of his power has not yet found a channel. If it remains without one, it will burn him up. At present he is unmarked by the dissipations in which he relieves his demoniac unrest; he has the fresh and shining look of an epic hero. He walks leisurely before the*

WINEMILLERS' *bench, negligently touching the crown of his hat but not glancing at them; climbs the steps to the base of the fountain, then turns and looks in the direction of the singer. A look of interest touched with irony appears on his face.*

A couple, strolling in the park, pass behind the fountain.]

THE GIRL: Look who's by the fountain!

THE MAN: Bright as a new silver dollar!

JOHN: Hi, Dusty! Hi, Pearl!

THE MAN: How'd you make out in that floating crap game?

JOHN: I floated with it as far as Vicksburg, then sank.

THE GIRL: Everybody's been calling: 'Johnny, Johnny — where's Johnny?'

[JOHN'S *father*, DR BUCHANAN, *comes on from right, as the* REV. *and* MRS WINEMILLER *move off the scene to left, towards the band music.* DR BUCHANAN *is an elderly man whose age shows in his slow and stiff movements. He walks with a cane.* JOHN *sees him coming, but pretends not to and starts to walk off.*]

DR BUCHANAN: *John!*

JOHN: Oh! Hi, Dad ...

[*The men stare at each other for a long tense moment. Finally* JOHN *speaks awkwardly.*]

I – uh – meant to wire you but I must've forgot. I got tied up in Vicksburg Saturday and just now got back to town ... I haven't been to the house yet ... Is – everything – O.K.?

DR BUCHANAN [*hoarsely with mounting fury*]: I left you in charge of my practice for the week-end. While I was gone, what happened?

JOHN: Oh Dad, you know what happened.

DR BUCHANAN: Yes, I know what happened. A woman died of a haemorrhage ...

JOHN: It was a terminal case of –

DR BUCHANAN: Be quiet, God damn you!

[JOHN *turns away.*]

Stay here! And listen to me. There is no room in the medical profession for wasters – drunkards – lechers!

JOHN: All right, then, let me out of it!

DR BUCHANAN: You were never in it! A medical diploma don't make you a doctor. No doctor fit to be called one would show that sort of – criminal irresponsibility towards his –

JOHN [*shouting*]: *Then let me out of it!*

DR BUCHANAN: I've sent your things to the Alhambra Hotel. [*Starts to go.*]

JOHN: Dad! I was with the old lady from seven till three in the morning. When she – lapsed into coma, I went out for some air. I saw the death of my mother, and ever since then I've had a dread of it that makes me unsuitable material for a doctor. I'm made for the science of medicine but not the practice of it.

DR BUCHANAN: I need you here, for a while. Pick up your things at the Alhambra Hotel, John – and bring them back to the house.

JOHN: – Yes, sir ...

DR BUCHANAN: I have to call on a patient. [*Nods slightly and goes off upper right.*]

[JOHN *looks after him with a faint, affectionate smile, then sits down on the steps with an air of relief, handkerchief to forehead, and a whistle of relief.*

MRS WINEMILLER *comes in from left, followed by her husband.*]

MRS WINEMILLER: Where is the ice-cream man?

MR WINEMILLER: Mother, hush! [*Just then the song ends. There is applause. Then the band strikes up the Santiago Waltz. He sees his daughter approaching.*] Here we are, Alma!

[ALMA WINEMILLER *enters.* ALMA *had an adult quality as a child, and now, in her middle twenties, there is something prematurely spinsterish about her. An excessive propriety and self-consciousness is apparent in her nervous laughter; her voice and gestures belong to years of church entertainments, to the position of hostess in a rectory. People her own age regard her as rather quaintly and humorously affected. She has grown up mostly in the company of her elders. Her true nature is still hidden even from herself. She is dressed in pale yellow and carries a yellow silk parasol.*

As ALMA *passes in front of the fountain,* JOHN *slaps his hands resoundingly together a few times. She catches her breath in a slight laughing sound, makes as if to retreat, with a startled 'Oh', but then goes quickly to her parents. The applause from the crowd continues.*]

MR WINEMILLER: They seem to want to hear you sing again, Alma.
[ALMA *turns nervously about, touching her throat and her chest.* JOHN *grins, applauding by the fountain. When the applause dies out,* ALMA *sinks faintly on the bench.*]

ALMA: Open my bag, Father. My fingers have frozen stiff! [*She draws a deep laboured breath.*] I don't know what came over me – absolute panic! Never, never again, it isn't worth it – the tortures that I go through!

MR WINEMILLER [*anxiously*]: You're having one of your nervous attacks?

ALMA: My heart's beating so! It seemed to be in my *throat* the whole time I was singing!
[JOHN *laughs audibly from the fountain.*]
Was it noticeable, Father?

MR WINEMILLER: You sang extremely well, Alma. But you know how I feel about this, it was contrary to my wishes and I cannot imagine why you wanted to do it, especially since it seemed to upset you so.

ALMA: I don't see how anyone could object to my singing at a patriotic occasion. If I had just sung well! But I barely got through it. At one point I thought that I wouldn't. The words flew out of my mind. Did you notice the pause? Blind panic! They really never came back, but I went on singing – I think I must have been improvising the lyric! Whew! Is there a handkerchief in it?

MRS WINEMILLER [*suddenly*]: Where is the ice-cream man?

ALMA [*rubbing her fingers together*]: Circulation is slowly coming back ...

MR WINEMILLER: Sit back quietly and take a deep breath, Alma.

ALMA: Yes, my handkerchief – now ...

MRS WINEMILLER: Where is the ice-cream man?

MR WINEMILLER: Mother, there isn't any ice-cream man.

ALMA: No, there isn't any ice-cream man, Mother. But on the way home Mr Doremus and I will stop by the drug store and pick up a pint of ice-cream.

MR WINEMILLER: Are you intending to stay here?

ALMA: Until the concert is over. I promised Roger I'd wait for him.

MR WINEMILLER: I suppose you have noticed who is by the fountain?

ALMA: *Shhh!*

MR WINEMILLER: Hadn't you better wait on a different bench?

ALMA: This is where Roger will meet me.

MR WINEMILLER: Well, Mother, we'll run along now.

[MRS WINEMILLER *has started vaguely towards the fountain,* MR WINEMILLER *firmly restraining her.*]

This way, this way, Mother! [*He takes arm and leads her off.*]

MRS WINEMILLER [*calling back, in a childish voice*]: Strawberry, Alma. Chocolate, chocolate and strawberry mixed! Not vanilla!

ALMA [*faintly*]: Yes, yes, Mother – vanilla . . .

MRS WINEMILLER [*furiously*]: I said *not* vanilla. [*Shouting.*] Strawberry!

MR WINEMILLER [*fiercely*]: Mother! We're attracting attention. [*He propels her forcibly away.*]

[JOHN *laughs by the fountain.* ALMA *moves her parasol so that it shields her face from him. She leans back, closing her eyes.* JOHN *notices a firecracker by the fountain. He leans over negligently to pick it up. He grins and lights it and tosses it towards* ALMA'*s bench. When it goes off she springs up with a shocked cry, letting the parasol drop.*]

JOHN [*jumping up as if outraged*]: Hey! Hey, you!

[*He looks off to right.* ALMA *sinks back weakly on the bench.* JOHN *solicitously advances.*]

Are you all right?

ALMA: I can't seem to – catch my breath! Who threw it?

JOHN: Some little rascal.

ALMA: Where?

JOHN: He ran away quick when I hollered!

ALMA: There ought to be an ordinance passed in this town forbidding firecrackers.

JOHN: Dad and I treated fifteen kids for burns the last couple of days. I think you need a little restorative, don't you? [*He takes out a flask.*] Here!

ALMA: What is it?

JOHN: Apple-jack brandy.

ALMA: No thank you.

JOHN: Liquid dynamite.

ALMA: I'm sure.

[JOHN *laughs and returns it to his pocket. He remains looking down at* ALMA *with one foot on the end of her bench. His steady, smiling look into her face is disconcerting her.*

In ALMA'S *voice and manner there is a delicacy and elegance, a kind of 'airiness', which is really natural to her, as it is, in a less marked degree, to many Southern girls. Her gestures and mannerisms are a bit exaggerated but in a graceful way. It is understandable that she might be accused of 'putting on airs' and being 'affected' by the other young people of the town. She seems to belong to a more elegant age, such as the eighteenth century in France. Out of nervousness and self-consciousness she has a habit of prefacing and concluding her remarks with a little breathless laugh. This will be indicated at points, but should be used more freely than indicated; however, the characterization must never be stressed to the point of making her at all ludicrous in a less sympathetic way.*]

ALMA: You're – home for the summer?

[JOHN *gives an affirmative grunt.*]

Summer is not the pleasantest time of year to renew an acquaintance with Glorious Hill – is it?

[JOHN *gives an indefinite grunt.* ALMA *laughs airily.*]

The Gulf wind has failed us this year, disappointed us dreadfully this summer. We used to be able to rely on the Gulf wind to cool the nights off for us, but this summer has been an exceptional season.

[JOHN *continues to grin disconcertingly down at* ALMA; *she shows her discomfiture in flurried gestures.*]

JOHN [*slowly*]: Are you – disturbed about something?

ALMA: That firecracker was a shock.

JOHN: You should be over that shock by now.

ALMA: I don't get over shocks quickly.

JOHN: I see you don't.

ALMA: You're planning to stay here and take over some of your father's medical practice?

JOHN: I haven't made up my mind about anything yet.

ALMA: I hope so, we all hope so. Your father was telling me that you have succeeded in isolating the germ of that fever epidemic that's broken out at Lyon.

JOHN: Finding something to kill it is more of a trick.

ALMA: You'll do that! He's so positive that you will. He says that you made a special study of bacter ... bacter ...

JOHN: Bacteriology!

ALMA: Yes! At Johns Hopkins! That's in Boston, isn't it?

JOHN: No. Baltimore.

ALMA: Oh, Baltimore. Baltimore, Maryland. Such a beautiful combination of names. And bacteriology — isn't that something you do with a microscope?

JOHN: Well — partly ...

ALMA: I've looked through a telescope, but never a microscope. What ... what do you — see?

JOHN: A — universe, Miss Alma.

ALMA: What kind of a universe?

JOHN: Pretty much the same kind that you saw through the lens of a telescope — a mysterious one ...

ALMA: Oh, yes ...

JOHN: Part anarchy — and part order!

ALMA: The footprints of God!

JOHN: But not God.

ALMA [*ecstatically*]: To be a doctor! And deal with these mysteries under the microscope lens ... I think it is more religious than being a priest! There is so much suffering in the world it actually makes one sick to think about it, and most of us are so helpless to relieve it ... But a physician! Oh, my! With his magnificent gifts and training what a joy it must be to know that he is equipped and appointed to bring relief to all of this fearful suffering — and fear! And it's an expanding profession; it's a profession that is continually widening its horizons. So many diseases have already come under scientific control but the commencement is just — beginning! I mean there is so much more that is yet to be done, such as mental afflictions to be brought under control ... And with your father's example to inspire you! Oh, my!

JOHN: I didn't know you had so many ideas about the medical profession.

ALMA: Well, I am a great admirer of your father, as well as a patient. It's such a comfort knowing that he's right next door, within arm's reach as it were!

JOHN: Why? Do you have fits? . . .

ALMA: Fits? [*She throws back her head with a peal of gay laughter.*] Why no, but I do have attacks! – of nervous heart trouble. Which can be so alarming that I run straight to your father!

JOHN: At two or three in the morning?

ALMA: Yes, as late as that, even . . . occasionally. He's very patient with me.

JOHN: But does you no good?

ALMA: He always reassures me.

JOHN: Temporarily?

ALMA: Yes . . .

JOHN: Don't you want more than that?

ALMA: What?

JOHN: It's none of my business.

ALMA: What were you going to say?

JOHN: You're Dad's patient. But I have an idea . . .

ALMA: Please go on!

[JOHN *laughs a little.*]

Now you have to go on! You can't leave me up in the air! What were you going to tell me?

JOHN: Only that I suspect you need something more than a little temporary reassurance.

ALMA: *Why?* You think it's more serious than . . . ?

JOHN: You're swallowing air, Miss Alma.

ALMA: I'm what?

JOHN: You're swallowing air, Miss Alma.

ALMA: I'm swallowing air?

JOHN: Yes, you swallow air when you laugh or talk. It's a little trick that hysterical women get into.

ALMA [*uncertainly*]: Ha-ha . . . !

JOHN: You swallow air and it presses on your heart and gives you

128

palpitations. That isn't serious in itself but it's a symptom of something that is. Shall I tell frankly?

ALMA: Yes!

JOHN: Well, what I think you have is a *doppelganger*! You have a *doppelganger* and the *doppelganger* is badly irritated.

ALMA: Oh, my goodness! I have an irritated *doppelganger*! [*She tries to laugh, but is definitely uneasy*.] How awful that sounds! What exactly *is* it?

JOHN: It's none of *my* business. You are not *my* patient.

ALMA: But that's downright wicked of you! To tell me I have something awful-sounding as that, and then refuse to let me know what it is! [*She tries to laugh again, unsuccessfully*.]

JOHN: I shouldn't have said anything! I'm not your doctor ...

ALMA: Just how did you arrive at this – diagnosis of my case? [*She laughs*.] But of course you're teasing me. Aren't you? ... There, the Gulf wind is stirring! He's actually moving the leaves of the palmetto! And listen to them complaining ...

[*As if brought in by this courier from the tropics,* ROSA GONZALES *enters and crosses to the fountain. Her indolent walk produces a sound and an atmosphere like the Gulf wind on the palmettos, a whispering of silk and a slight rattle of metallic ornaments. She is dressed in an almost outrageous finery, with lustrous feathers on her hat, greenish blue, a cascade of them, also diamond and emerald earrings.*]

JOHN [*sharply*]: *Who is that?*

ALMA: I'm surprised that you don't know.

JOHN: I've been away quite a while.

ALMA: That's the Gonzales girl ... Her father's the owner of the gambling casino on Moon Lake.

[ROSA *drinks at the fountain and wanders leisurely off.*]

She smiled at you, didn't she?

JOHN: I thought she did.

ALMA: I hope that you have a strong character.

[JOHN *places a foot on the end of the bench.*]

JOHN: Solid rock.

ALMA [*nervously*]: The pyrotechnical display is going to be brilliant.

JOHN: The what?

ALMA: The fireworks.

JOHN: Aw!

ALMA: I suppose you've lost touch with most of your *old* friends here.

JOHN: [*laconically*]: Yeah.

ALMA: You must make some *new* ones! I belong to a little group that meets every ten days. I think you'd enjoy them, too. They're young people with – intellectual and artistic interests . . .

JOHN [*sadly*]: Aw, I see . . . intellectual . . .

ALMA: You must come! – sometime – I'm going to remind you of it . . .

JOHN: Thanks. Do you mind if I sit down?

ALMA: Why, certainly not, there's room enough for two! Neither of us are – terribly large in diameter! [*She laughs shrilly.*]

[*A girl's voice is heard calling: 'Good-bye, Nellie!' and another answers: 'Good-bye!'* NELLIE EWELL *enters – a girl of sixteen with a radiantly fresh healthy quality.*]

Here comes someone much nicer! One of my adorable little vocal pupils, the youngest and prettiest one with the least gift for music.

JOHN: I know that one.

ALMA: Hello, there, Nellie dear!

NELLIE: Oh, Miss Alma, your singing was so beautiful it made me cry.

ALMA: It's sweet of you to fib so. I sang terribly.

NELLIE: You're just being modest, Miss Alma. Hello, Dr John! Dr John!

JOHN: Yeah?

NELLIE: That book you gave me is too full of long words.

JOHN: Look 'em up in the dictionary, Nellie.

NELLIE: I did, but you know how dictionaries are. You look up one long word and it gives you another long word and you look up that long word and it gives you the long word you looked up in the first place.

[JOHN *laughs.*]

I'm coming over tomorrow for you to explain it all to me. [*She laughs and goes off.*]

ALMA: What book is she talking about?

JOHN: A book I gave her about the facts of nature. She came over to the office and told me her mother wouldn't tell her anything and she had to know because she'd fallen in love.

ALMA: Why the precocious little – imp! [*She laughs.*]

JOHN: What sort of a mother has she?

ALMA: Mrs Ewell's the merry widow of Glorious Hill. They say that she goes to the depot to meet every train in order to make the acquaintance of travelling salesmen. Of course she is ostracized by all but a few of her own type of women in town, which is terribly hard for Nellie. It isn't fair to the child. Father didn't want me to take her as a pupil because of her mother's reputation, but I feel that one has a duty to perform towards children in such – circumstances … And I always say that life is such a mysteriously complicated thing that no one should really presume to judge and condemn the behaviour of anyone else!

[*There is a faraway 'puff' and a burst of golden light over their heads. Both look up. There is a long-drawn 'Ahhh …' from the invisible crowd. This is an effect that will be repeated at intervals during the scene.*]

There goes the first skyrocket! Oh, look at it burst into a million stars!

[*JOHN leans way back to look up and allow his knees to spread wide apart so that one of them is in contact with ALMA's. The effect upon her is curiously disturbing.*]

JOHN [*after a moment*]: Do you have a chill?

ALMA: Why, no! – no. Why?

JOHN: You're shaking.

ALMA: Am I?

JOHN: Don't you feel it?

ALMA: I have a touch of malaria lingering on.

JOHN: You have malaria?

ALMA: Never severely, never really severely. I just have touches of it that come and go. [*She laughs airily.*]

JOHN [*with a gentle grin*]: Why do you laugh that way?

ALMA: What way?

[*JOHN imitates her laugh. ALMA laughs again in embarrassment.*]

JOHN: Yeah. That way.

ALMA: I do declare, you haven't changed in the slightest. It used to delight you to embarrass me and it still does!

JOHN: I guess I shouldn't tell you this, but I heard an imitation of you at a party.

ALMA: Imitation? Of what?

JOHN: You.

ALMA: I? – I? Why, *what* did they imitate?

JOHN: You singing at a wedding.

ALMA: My voice?

JOHN: Your gestures and facial expression! Some people have got the idea you're a little bit affected.

ALMA: How mystifying!

JOHN: No, I shouldn't have told you. You're upset about it.

ALMA: I'm not in the least upset, I am just mystified. Who gave this imitation at this party you spoke of?

JOHN [*grinning*]: I don't think she'd want that told.

ALMA: Oh, it was a *she* then?

JOHN: You don't think a man could do it?

ALMA: No, and I don't think a lady would do it either!

JOHN: I didn't think it would have made you so mad, or I wouldn't have brought it up.

ALMA: Oh, I'm not mad. I'm just mystified and amazed, as I always am by unprovoked malice in people. These people who call me affected and give these unkind imitations of me – I wonder if they stop to think that my circumstances are somewhat different from theirs? My father and I have a certain – cross – to bear!

JOHN: What cross?

ALMA: Living next door to us, you should know what cross.

JOHN: Mrs Winemiller?

ALMA: Almost immediately after my father was ordained into the Ministry she started slipping back into her childhood to escape the responsibilities of a rectory. I had to take over those responsibilities at an early age, and that may have made me seem strange to some of my more critical contemporaries.

[*Another rocket goes up. Another 'Ahhh ...' from the crowd.*]

JOHN: You ought to go out with young people.

ALMA: I am not a recluse. I don't fly around here and there giving imitations of other people at parties. But I am not a recluse by any manner of means.

JOHN: I have seen you in the public library and the park, but only two or three times have I seen you out with a boy and it was always someone like this Roger Doremus.

ALMA: I'm afraid that you and I move in different circles. If I wished to be as outspoken as you are, which is sometimes just an excuse for being rude – I might say that I've yet to see you in the company of a – well, a – reputable young woman. And the pity of it is that you are preparing to be a doctor. You're intending to practise your father's profession here in Glorious Hill. [*She catches her breath in a sob.*] While he is devoting himself to the fever at Lyon you drive your automobile at a reckless pace from one disorderly roadhouse to another! And you – a gifted young doctor – *Magna cum Laude!* [*She turns aside, touching her eyelids with a handkerchief.*] You know what I call it? I call it a *desecration!*

[ALMA *sobs uncontrollably. Then she springs up from the bench.* JOHN *catches her hand.*]

JOHN: You're not going to run off, are you?

ALMA: Singing in public always – always upsets me! – Let go of my hand.

[JOHN *holds on to it, grinning up at* ALMA *in the deepening dusk. The stars are coming out in the cyclorama with its leisurely floating cloud-forms. In the distance the band is playing 'La Golondrina'.*]

Please let go of my hand.

JOHN: Don't run off mad.

ALMA: Let's not make a spectacle of ourselves.

JOHN: Then sit back down.

[*A skyrocket goes up. The crowd 'Ahhh ... s'.*]

ALMA: You threw that firecracker and started a conversation just in order to tease me as you did as a child. You came to this bench in order to embarrass me and to hurt my feelings with the report of that vicious – imitation! No, let go of my hand so I can leave, now. You've succeeded in your purpose. I *was* hurt! I *did* make a fool of myself as you intended! So let me go now!

JOHN: You're attracting attention! Don't you know that I really *like* you, Miss Alma?

ALMA: No, you don't.

[*Another skyrocket.*]

JOHN: Sure I do. A lot. Sometimes when I come home late at night I look over at the rectory. I see something white at the window. Could that be you, Miss Alma? Or, is it your *doppelganger*, looking out of the window that faces my way?

ALMA: Enough about *doppelganger* – whatever that is!

JOHN: There goes a nice one, roman candle they call it!

[*This time the explosion is in back of them. A roman candle shoots up puffs of rainbow-coloured light in back of the stone angel of the fountain. They turn in profile to watch it.*]

JOHN [*counting the puffs of light*]: Four – five – six – that's all? No – seven!

[*There is a pause.* ALMA *sits down slowly.*]

ALMA [*vaguely*]: Dear me ... [*She fans herself.*]

JOHN: How about going riding?

ALMA [*too eagerly*]: When ... now?

[ROSA GONZALES *has wandered up to the fountain again.* JOHN's *attention drifts steadily towards her and away from* ALMA.]

JOHN [*too carelessly*]: Oh ... some afternoon.

ALMA: Would you observe the speed limit?

JOHN: Strictly with you, Miss Alma.

ALMA: Why then, I'd be glad to – John.

[JOHN *has risen from the bench and crosses to the fountain.*]

JOHN: And wear a hat with a plume!

ALMA: I don't have a hat with a plume!

JOHN: Get one!

[*Another skyrocket goes up, and there is another long 'Ahhh ...' from the crowd.* JOHN *saunters up to the fountain.* ROSA *has lingered beside it. As he passes her he whispers something. She laughs and moves leisurely off.* JOHN *takes a quick drink at the fountain, then follows* ROSA, *calling back 'good night' to* ALMA. *There is a sound of laughter in the distance.* ALMA *sits motionless for a moment, then touches a small*

white handkerchief to her lips and nostrils. MR DOREMUS *comes in,*
carrying a French horn case. He is a small man, somewhat like a
sparrow.]

ROGER: *Whew! Golly! Moses!* – Well, how did it go, Miss Alma?

ALMA: How did – what – go?

ROGER [*annoyed*]: My solo on the French horn.

ALMA [*slowly, without thinking*]: I paid no attention to it. [*She rises*
slowly and takes his arm.] I'll have to hang on your arm – I'm feeling
so dizzy!

[*The scene dims out. There is a final skyrocket and a last 'Ahhh ...'*
from the crowd in the distance. Music is heard, and there is light on the
angel.]

SCENE II

The Winemillers' parlour.

MRS WINEMILLER *enters from the inside door. She is carrying her parasol,*
from the folds of which she removes a hat with billowing white plumes.
Looking in the mirror, she places the hat on her head.

MRS WINEMILLER:

If I wore a tall hat in a sunny room,
I would sweep the ceiling with a cavalier's plume!

If I wore a velvet cloak along the esplanade
I'd fascinate an officer in red and gold brocade!

If I spoke behind a fan on a white verandah
I would shock a simple heart with my heartless candour!
Ha ha ha ha!

[*The telephone rings.* MRS WINEMILLER *snatches off the hat, hides it*
under the centre table, and quickly sits at the table and works on her
picture puzzle. The telephone goes on ringing. ALMA *comes in to*
answer it.]

ALMA: Hello ... Yes, Mr Gillam ... She did? ... Are you sure? ...
How shocking! ...

[MRS WINEMILLER *now retrieves the hat and puts it on.*]

Thank you, Mr Gillam ... the hat is here.

[MR WINEMILLER *comes in through the inside door. He is distracted.*]

135

MR WINEMILLER: Alma! Alma, your mother ... !

ALMA: I know, Father, Mr Gillam just phoned. He told me she picked up a white plumed hat and he pretended not to notice in order to save you the embarrassment, so I – I told him to just charge it to us.

MR WINEMILLER: That hat looks much too expensive.

ALMA: It's fourteen dollars. You pay six of it, Father, and I'll pay eight.

MR WINEMILLER: What an insufferable cross we have to bear.

[*He retires despairingly from the room, through the inner door.*]

ALMA: I have a thousand and one things to do before my club meeting tonight, so you work quietly on your picture puzzle or I shall take the hat back, plume and all.

MRS WINEMILLER [*throwing pieces of the puzzle on the floor*]: The pieces don't fit!

[ALMA *picks up the pieces and puts them on the table.*]

The pieces don't fit!

[ALMA *stands for a moment looking at the hat. She reaches for the phone, then puts it down. Then she picks it up again, and asks for 'ELM 362'. The telephone across the way in the doctor's office rings and that part of the scene lights up.* JOHN *comes in.*]

JOHN [*answering the phone*]: Hello

ALMA: John! [*She fans herself rapidly with a palm leaf clutched in her free hand and puts on a brilliant, strained smile as if she were actually in his presence.*]

JOHN [*sitting on the desk and, during the conversation, mixing a bromo*]: Miss Alma?

ALMA: You recognized my voice?

JOHN: I recognized your laugh.

ALMA: Ha-ha! How are you, you stranger you?

JOHN: I'm pretty well, Miss Alma. How're you doing?

ALMA: Surviving, just surviving! Isn't it fearful?

JOHN: Uh-huh.

ALMA: You seem unusually laconic. Or perhaps I should say more than usually laconic.

JOHN: I was at Moon Lake Casino last night and I'm just recovering from it.

ALMA: Well, sir, I have a bone to pick with you!

JOHN: What's that, Miss Alma? [*He drains the glass of bromo.*]

ALMA: The time of our last conversation on the Fourth of July, you said you were going to take me riding in your automobile.

JOHN: Aw. Did I say that?

ALMA: Yes indeed you did, sir! And all these hot afternoons I've been breathlessly waiting and hoping that you would remember that promise. But now I know how insincere you are. Ha-ha!

MRS WINEMILLER: Ha ha ha!

ALMA: Time and again the four-wheeled phenomenon flashes by the rectory and I have yet to put my – my quaking foot in it.

MRS WINEMILLER: Quaking foot in it. Ha-ha! Four-wheeled phenomenon.

JOHN: What was that, Miss Alma! I didn't understand you.

ALMA: I was just reprimanding you, sir! Castigating you verbally! Ha-ha!

JOHN: What about, Miss Alma?

ALMA: Never mind. I know how busy you are.

MRS WINEMILLER: She's busy.

ALMA [*whispers*]: Mother, *hush!*

JOHN: I'm afraid we have a bad connection.

ALMA: I hate telephones. I don't know why, but they always make me laugh as if someone were poking me in the ribs! I swear to goodness they do!

JOHN: Why don't you just go to your window and I'll go to mine and we can holler across?

ALMA: The yard's so wide I'm afraid it would crack my voice! And I've got to sing at somebody's wedding tomorrow.

JOHN: You're going to sing at a wedding?

ALMA: Yes. 'The Voice that Breathed o'er Eden!' And I'm as hoarse as a frog! [*Another gale of laughter almost shakes her off her feet.*]

JOHN: Better come over and let me give you a gargle.

ALMA: Nasty gargles – I hate them!

MRS WINEMILLER [*mockingly*]: Nasty gargles – I hate them!

ALMA: Mother, shhh! – please! As you no doubt have gathered, there is some interference at this end of the line! What I wanted to say is –

you remember my mentioning that little club I belong to?

JOHN: Aw! Aw, yes! Those cultural meetings!

ALMA: Oh, now, don't call it that. It's just a little informal gathering every Wednesday and we talk about the new books and read things out loud to each other!

JOHN: Serve any refreshments?

ALMA: Yes, we serve refreshments!

JOHN: Any liquid refreshments?

ALMA: Both liquid and solid refreshments.

JOHN: Is this an invitation?

ALMA: Didn't I promise I'd ask you? It's going to be tonight! – at eight at my house, at the rectory, so all you'll have to do is cross the yard!

JOHN: I'll try to make it, Miss Alma.

ALMA: Don't say try as if it required some Herculean effort! All you have to do is ...

JOHN: Cross the yard! Uh-huh – reserve me a seat by the punchbowl.

ALMA: That gives me an idea! We *will* have punch, fruit punch, with claret in it. Do you like claret?

JOHN: I just dote on claret.

ALMA: Now you're being sarcastic! Ha-ha-ha!

JOHN: Excuse me, Miss Alma, but Dad's got to use this phone.

ALMA: I won't hang up till you've said you'll come without fail!

JOHN: I'll be there, Miss Alma. You can count on it.

ALMA: Au revoir, then! Until eight.

JOHN: G'bye, Miss Alma.

[JOHN *hangs up with an incredulous grin.* ALMA *remains holding the phone with a dazed smile until the office interior has dimmed slowly out.*]

MRS WINEMILLER: Alma's in love, Alma's in lo-ove!

ALMA [*sharply*]: Mother, you are wearing out my patience.

[NELLIE *rings the bell.* ALMA *answers it.*]

Oh, it's you, Nellie. Go straight to the piano, Nellie, and practise your scales while I go find the punchbowl for my club meeting.

[ALMA *leads* NELLIE *to the piano, then exits through the inner door.* NELLIE *sings a scale.* MRS WINEMILLER *imitates her. During the imitation* ALMA *re-enters with the punchbowl and crosses to the love seat.*]

ALMA: Mother, you're interrupting the lesson.

NELLIE: Oh, Miss Alma, I don't feel like taking a lesson today.

ALMA: Frankly, Nellie, I don't understand why you wanted to take vocal lessons at all.

NELLIE [*cheerfully*]: I don't have a voice, Miss Alma?

ALMA: Yes, you do have a voice but your voice is better for – speaking.

NELLIE: Don't you know why I took lessons?

ALMA: I'm afraid I don't.

NELLIE: I had a crush on you!

ALMA: On *me*?

NELLIE: You know what crushes are?

ALMA: Oh, yes, but – why on me?

NELLIE: Because you've been nice to me in spite of Mother's reputation.

ALMA: – Both of us – have – mothers . . .

NELLIE: Yes, but yours doesn't go to the depot at midnight to meet the travelling salesman that get off the Cannonball Express!

ALMA: No . . . Mine doesn't do *that*!

DUSTY [*off*]: Johnny!

NELLIE: Anyway, I had a crush on you. Those were the days when I had crushes on girls, but those days are over with now and I – have crushes on – *boys* . . .

ALMA: I hope that you will be sensible about them.

DUSTY [*off*]: Johnny!

ALMA: What are you doing at the window, Nellie?

NELLIE: Watching someone I have a *terrible* crush on!

ALMA: Someone – next door?

NELLIE: You know who – Dr Johnny, Junior. You know, I thought I'd always hate men. Loathe and despise them. But now, oh, I think he's the wonderfullest person in all the world. Don't you think so?

ALMA: In appearance perhaps, but his character is weak. Where do you see him? [*She catches* MRS WINEMILLER'S *eye.*]

NELLIE: He isn't dressed, so I think it must be his bedroom.

ALMA: Please come away from the window.

NELLIE: He's brushing his hair.

ALMA: Nellie, come away from that window.

DUSTY [*off*] Johnny! Johnny!

NELLIE: Someone's calling him.

ALMA: Yes, these people who shout his name in front of his house are of such a character that the old doctor cannot permit them to come inside the door. And when they have brought him home at night, left him sprawling on the front steps, sometimes at daybreak – it takes two people, his father and the old cook, one pushing and one pulling, to get him upstairs to bed.

A GIRL'S VOICE [*off*]: Johnny! Johnny!

NELLIE: They're calling again. There he is. He's getting into his shirt.

ALMA: Nellie, don't look out the window and have us caught spying.

MRS WINEMILLER [*suddenly*]: Show Nellie how *you* spy on him! Oh, she's a good one at spying. She stands behind the curtain and *peeks* around it, and . . .

ALMA [*frantically*]: *Mother!*

MRS WINEMILLER: She spies on him. Whenever he comes in at night she rushes downstairs to watch him out of this window!

ALMA [*interrupting her*]: Be still!

MRS WINEMILLER [*going right on*]: She called him just now and had a fit on the telephone!

[*The old lady cackles derisively.* ALMA *snatches her cigarette from her and crushes it under her foot.*]

ALMA: Nellie, Nellie, please go.

NELLIE [*with a startled giggle*]: All right, Miss Alma, I'm going. [*She crosses quickly to the door, looking back once with a grin.*] Good night, Mrs Winemiller!

[NELLIE *goes out, up the fountain steps.* MRS WINEMILLER *goes outside the door.*

MRS WINEMILLER: Alma's in love! Alma's in lo-ove!

[ALMA *drags* MRS WINEMILLER *inside and forces her on to the fender seat.*]

ALMA: If ever I hear you say such a thing again, if ever you dare to repeat such a thing in my presence or anybody else's – then it will

be the last straw! You understand me? Yes, you undersantd me!
You act like a child, but you have the devil in you. And God will
punish you – yes! I'll punish you too. I'll take your cigarettes from
you and give you no more. I'll give you no ice-cream either.
Because I'm tired of your malice, yes. I'm tired of your malice and
your self-indulgence. People wonder why I'm tied down here!
They pity me – think of me as an old maid already! In spite of
I'm young. Still young! It's you – it's you, you've taken my
youth away from me! I wouldn't say that – I'd try not even to think
of it – if you were just kind, just simple! But I could spread my
life out like a rug for you to step on and you'd step on it, and not
even say 'Thank you, Alma!' Which is what you've done always –
and now you dare to tell a disgusting lie about me – in front of
that girl!

MRS WINEMILLER: What lie, what lie do you mean?

ALMA [*seizing the hat from* MRS WINEMILLER'*s head*]: Give me that
hat, Mother. It goes back.

MRS WINEMILLER [*lunges at the hat*]: *Fight! Fight!*

[ALMA *snatches at the plumed hat.* MRS WINEMILLER *snatches, too.*
The hat is torn between them.]

ALMA: Upstairs, Mother!

MRS WINEMILLER [*retreats to the inner door*]: Can I have some ice-
cream?

ALMA: Upstairs, Mother

[MRS WINEMILLER *goes.*]

A hat with a plume.

SCENE III

Inside the rectory.
The meeting is in progress, having just opened with the reading of the
minutes by ALMA. *She stands before the green plush sofa and the others. This*
group includes MR DOREMUS, VERNON, *a willowy young man with an*
open collar and Byronic locks, the widow BASSETT, *and a wistful older girl*
with a long neck and thick-lensed glasses.

ALMA [*reading*]: Our last meeting which fell on July fourteenth ...

MRS BASSETT: Bastille Day!

ALMA: Pardon me?

MRS BASSETT: It fell on Bastille Day! But, honey, that was the meeting before last.

ALMA: You're perfectly right. I seem to be on the wrong page ... [*She drops the papers.*]

MRS BASSETT: Butterfingers!

ALMA: Here we are! July twenty-fifth! Correct?

MRS BASSETT: Correct!

[*A little ripple of laughter goes about the circle.*]

ALMA [*continuing*]: It was debated whether or not we ought to suspend operations for the remainder of the summer as the departure of several members engaged in the teaching profession for their summer vacations ...

MRS BASSETT: Lucky people!

ALMA: ... had substantially contracted our little circle.

MRS BASSETT: Decimated our ranks!

[*There is another ripple of laughter.*

JOHN *appears outside the door-frame and rings the bell.*]

ALMA [*with agitation*]: Is that – is that – the doorbell?

MRS BASSETT: It sure did sound like it to me.

ALMA: Excuse me a moment. I think it may be ...

[ALMA *crosses to the door-frame and makes the gesture of opening the door.* JOHN *steps in, immaculately groomed and shining, his white linen coat over his arm and a white Panama hat in his hand. He is a startling contrast to the other male company, who seem to be outcasts of a state in which he is a prominent citizen.*]

ALMA [*shrilly*]: Yes, it is – our guest of honour! Everbody, this is Dr John Buchanan, Junior.

JOHN [*easily glancing about the assemblage*]: Hello, everybody. [*To* ALMA] Did I miss much?

ROSEMARY: Good evening.

MRS BASSETT: Why, Dr John!

ALMA: Not a thing! Just the minutes – I'll put you on the sofa. Next to me.

MRS BASSETT: I never thought he'd show up. Congratulations, Miss
Alma.

[ALMA *laughs breathlessly and makes an uncertain gesture.* JOHN
*settles gingerly on the sofa. They all stare at him with a curious sort of
greediness.*]

ALMA: Well, now! we are completely assembled!

MRS BASSETT [*eagerly*]: Vernon has his verse play with him tonight!

ALMA [*uneasily*]: Is that right, Vernon?

[*Obviously it is.* VERNON *has a pile of papers eight inches thick on his
knees. He raises them timidly with downcast eyes.*]

ROGER [*quickly*]: We decided to put that off till cooler weather. Miss
Rosemary is supposed to read us a paper tonight on William
Blake.

MRS BASSETT: Those dead poets can keep!

[JOHN *laughs.*]

ALMA [*excitedly jumping up*]: Mrs Bassett, everybody! This is the way I
feel about the verse play. It's too important a thing to read under
any but ideal circumstances. Not only atmospheric – on some cool
evening with music planned to go with it! – but everyone present
so that nobody will miss it! Why don't we . . .

ROGER: Why don't we take a standing vote on the matter?

ALMA: Good, good, perfect!

ROGER: All in favour of putting the verse play off till cooler weather,
stand up!

[*Everybody rises but* ROSEMARY *and* MRS BASSETT. ROSEMARY
starts vaguely to rise, but MRS BASSETT *jerks her arm.*]

ROSEMARY: Was this a vote?

ROGER: Now, Mrs Bassett, no rough tactics, please!

ALMA: Has everybody got fans? John, you haven't got one!

[ALMA *looks about for a fan for* JOHN. *Not seeing one, she takes*
ROGER's *out of his hand and gives it to* JOHN. ROGER *is nonplussed.*
ROSEMARY *gets up with her paper.*]

ROSEMARY: The poet – William Blake was born in 1757. Visionary
he was, but certainly not demented.

MRS BASSETT: Insane, insane; that man was a mad fanatic!

[MRS BASSETT *squints her eyes tight shut and thrusts her thumbs into her ears. The reactions range from indignant to conciliatory.*]

ROGER: Now, Mrs Bassett!

MRS BASSETT: This is a free country. I can speak my opinion. And I have *read up* on him. Go on, Rosemary. I wasn't criticizing your paper.

[*But* ROSEMARY *sits down, hurt.*]

ALMA: Mrs Bassett is only joking, Rosemary.

ROSEMARY: No, I don't want to read it if she feels that strongly about it.

MRS BASSETT: Not a bit, don't be silly! I just don't see why we should encourage the writings of people like that who have already gone into a drunkard's grave!

VERNON: Drunkard's?

VARIOUS VOICES [*exclaiming*]: Did he? I never heard that about him. Is that true?

ALMA: Mrs Bassett is mistaken about that. Mrs Bassett, you have confused Blake with someone else.

MRS BASSETT [*positively*]: Oh, no, don't tell me. I've read up on him and know what I'm talking about. He travelled around with a Frenchman who took a shot at him and landed them both in jail! Brussels, Brussels!

ROGER [*gaily*]: Brussels sprouts!

MRS BASSETT: That's where it happened, fired a gun at him in a drunken stupor, and later one of them died of T.B. in the gutter! All right. I'm finished. I won't say anything more. Go on with your paper, Rosemary. There's nothing like contact with culture!

[ALMA *gets up.*]

ALMA: Before Rosemary reads her paper on Blake, I think it would be a good idea, since some of us aren't acquainted with his work, to preface the critical and biographical comments with a reading of once of his loveliest lyric poems.

ROGER: Oh yes, Miss Alma.

[*Exclamations from others*].

ROSEMARY: I'm not going to read anything at all! Not I!

ALMA: Then let me read it then. [*She takes a paper from* ROSEMARY.]
... This is called 'Love's Secret'.

[ALMA *clears her throat and waits for a hush to settle.* ROSEMARY *looks stonily at the carpet.* MRS BASSETT *looks at the ceiling.* JOHN *coughs.*]

> Never seek to tell thy love,
> Love that never told can be,
> For the gentle wind doth move
> Silently, invisibly.
> I told my love, I told my love,
> I told him all my heart.
> Trembling, cold in ghastly fear
> Did my love depart.
> No sooner had he gone from me
> Than a stranger passing by,
> Silently, invisibly,
> Took him with a sigh!

[*There are various effusions and enthusiastic applause.*]

MRS BASSETT: Honey, you're right. That isn't the man I meant. I was thinking about the one who wrote about 'the bought red lips'. Who was it that wrote about the 'bought red lips'?

[JOHN *has risen abruptly. He signals to* ALMA *and points to his watch. He starts to leave.*]

ALMA [*springing up*]: John!

JOHN [*calling back*]: I have to call on a patient! Excuse me, everybody.

ALMA: Oh, John!

[ALMA *calls after him so sharply that the group is startled into silence.*]

ROSEMARY [*interpreting this as a cue to read her paper*]: 'The poet, William Blake, was born in 1757 . . .'

[ALMA *suddenly rushes to the door and goes out after* JOHN.]

ROGER: Of poor but honest parents.

MRS BASSETT: No supercilious comments out of you, sir. Go on, Rosemary. [*She speaks loudly.*] She has such a beautiful *voice*!

[ALMA *returns inside, looking stunned.*]

ALMA: Please excuse the interruption, Rosemary. Dr Buchanan had to call on a patient.

MRS BASSETT [*archly*]: I bet I know who the patient was. Ha-ha! That Gonzales girl whose father owns Moon Lake Casino and goes everywhere with two pistols strapped on his belt. Johnny Buchanan will get himself shot in that crowd!

ALMA: Why, Mrs Bassett, what gave you such an idea? I don't think that John even knows that Gonzales girl!

MRS BASSETT: He knows her, all right. In the biblical sense of the word, if you'll excuse me!

ALMA: No, I will not excuse you! A thing like that is inexcusable!

MRS BASSETT: Have you fallen for him, Miss Alma? Miss Alma has fallen for the young doctor! They tell me he has lots of new lady patients!

ALMA: Stop it! [*She stamps her foot furiously and crushes the palm leaf fan between her clenched hands.*] I won't have malicious talk here! You drove him away from the meeting after I'd bragged so much about how bright and interesting you all were! You put your worst foot forward and simpered and chattered and carried on like idiots, idiots! What am I saying? I – I – please excuse me! [*She rushes out of the inner door.*]

ROGER: I move that the meeting adjourn.

MRS BASSETT: I second the motion.

ROSEMARY: I don't understand – what happened?

MRS BASSETT: Poor Miss Alma! I'm afraid she's going just like her mother.

ROSEMARY: What a meeting!

[*They all go out.*

After a moment ALMA *re-enters with a tray of refreshments, looks about the deserted interior and bursts into hysterical laughter.*

The light dims out.]

In the doctor's office.

> JOHN *has a wound on his arm which he is bandaging with* ROSA'S *assistance.*

JOHN: Hold that end. Wrap it around. Pull it tight.

> [*There is a knock at the door. They look up silently. The knock is repeated.*]

I better answer before they wake up the old man.

> [JOHN *goes out. A few moments later he returns, followed by* ALMA. *He is rolling down his sleeve to conceal the bandage.* ALMA *stops short at the sight of* ROSA.]

Wait outside, Rosa. In the hall. But be quiet!

> [ROSA *gives* ALMA *a challenging look as she withdraws from the lighted area.* JOHN *explains about* ROSA.]

Miss Alma, a little emergency case.

ALMA: The patient you had to call on.

> [JOHN *grins.*]

I want to see your father.

JOHN: He's asleep. Anything I can do?

ALMA: No, I think not. I have to see your father.

JOHN: It's 2 a.m., Miss Alma.

ALMA: I know, I'm afraid I'll have to see him.

JOHN: What's the trouble?

> [*The voice of* JOHN'S FATHER *is heard, calling from above.*]

DR BUCHANAN: John! What's going on down there?

JOHN [*at the door*]: Nothing much, Dad. Somebody got cut in a fight.

DR BUCHANAN: I'm coming down.

JOHN: No. Don't! Stay in bed!

> [JOHN *rolls up his sleeve to show* ALMA *the bandaged wound. She gasps and touches her lips.*]

I've patched him up, Dad. You sleep! [*He executes the gesture of closing a door quietly on the hall.*]

ALMA: You've been in a brawl with that – woman!

> [JOHN *nods and rolls the sleeve back down.* ALMA *sinks faintly into a chair.*]

JOHN: Is your *doppelganger* cutting up again?

ALMA: It's your father I want to talk to.

JOHN: Be reasonable, Miss Alma. You're not that sick.

ALMA: Do you suppose I would come here at two o'clock in the morning if I were not seriously ill?

JOHN: It's no telling what you would do in a state of hysteria. [*He puts some powders in a glass of water.*] Toss that down, Miss Alma.

ALMA: What is it?

JOHN: A couple of little white tablets dissolved in water.

ALMA: What kind of tablets?

JOHN: You don't trust me?

ALMA: You are not in any condition to inspire much confidence. [JOHN *laughs softly.* ALMA *looks at him helplessly for a moment, then bursts into tears. He draws up a chair beside hers and puts his arm gently about her shoulders.*]

I seem to be all to pieces.

JOHN: The intellectual meeting wore you out.

ALMA: You made a quick escape from it.

JOHN: I don't like meetings. The only meetings I like are between two people.

ALMA: Such as between yourself and the lady outside?

JOHN: Or between you and me.

ALMA [*nervously*]: Where is the medicine?

JOHN: Oh. You've decided to take it?

ALMA: Yes, if you ...

[ALMA *sips and chokes.* JOHN *gives her his handkerchief. She touches her lips with it.*]

JOHN: Bitter?

ALMA: Awfully bitter.

JOHN: It'll make you sleepy.

ALMA: I do hope so. I wasn't able to sleep.

JOHN: And you felt panicky?

ALMA: Yes. I felt walled in.

JOHN: You started hearing your heart?

ALMA: Yes, like a drum!

JOHN: It scared you?

148

ALMA: It always does.

JOHN: Sure. I know.

ALMA: I don't think I will be able to get through the summer.

JOHN: You'll get through it, Miss Alma.

ALMA: How?

JOHN: One day will come after another and one night will come after another till sooner or later the summer will be all through with and then it will be fall, and you will be saying, I don't see how I'm going to get through the fall.

ALMA: Oh . . .

JOHN: That's right. Draw a deep breath!

ALMA: Ah . . .

JOHN: Good. Now draw another!

ALMA: Ah . . .

JOHN: Better? Better?

ALMA: A little.

JOHN: Soon you'll be much better. [*He takes out a big silver watch and holds her wrist.*] Did y'know that time is one side of the four-dimensional continuum we're caught in?

ALMA: What?

JOHN: Did you know space is curved, that it turns back on to itself like a soap-bubble, adrift in something that's even less than space? [*He laughs a little as he replaces the watch.*]

ROSA [*faintly from outside*]: Johnny!

JOHN [*looking up as if the cry came from there*]: Did you know that the Magellanic clouds are a hundred thousand light years away from the earth? No?

[ALMA *shakes her head slightly.*]

That's something to think about when you worry over your heart, that little red fist that's got to keep knocking, knocking against the big black door.

ROSA [*more distinctly*]: Johnny! [*She opens the door a crack.*]

JOHN: Calla de la boca [*The door closes and he speaks to* ALMA.] There's nothing wrong with your heart but a little functional disturbance, like I told you before. You want me to check it?

[ALMA *nods mutely.* JOHN *picks up his stethoscope.*]

149

ALMA: The lady outside, I hate to keep her waiting.

JOHN: Rosa doesn't mind waiting. Unbutton your blouse.

ALMA: Unbutton ... ?

JOHN: The blouse.

ALMA: Hadn't I better – better come back in the morning, when your father will be able to ... ?

JOHN: Just as you please, Miss Alma.

[ALMA *hesitates. Then begins to unbutton her blouse. Her fingers fumble.*]

Fingers won't work?

ALMA [*breathlessly*]: They are just as if frozen!

JOHN [*smiling*]: Let me. [*He leans over her.*] Little pearl buttons ...

ALMA: If your father discovered that woman in the house ...

JOHN: He won't discover it.

ALMA: It would distress him terribly.

JOHN: Are you going to tell him?

ALMA: Certainly not!

[JOHN *laughs and applies the stethoscope to her chest.*]

JOHN: Breathe! ... Out! ... Breathe! ... Out!

ALMA: Ah ...

JOHN: Um-hmmm ...

ALMA: What do you hear?

JOHN: Just a little voice saying: 'Miss Alma is lonesome!'

[ALMA *rises and turns her back to him.*]

ALMA: If your idea of helping a patient is to ridicule and insult ...

JOHN: My idea of helping you is to tell you the truth.

[ALMA *looks up at* JOHN. *He lifts her hand from the chair arm.*]
What is this stone?

ALMA: A topaz.

JOHN: Beautiful stone ... Fingers still frozen?

ALMA: A little.

[JOHN *lifts her hand to his mouth and blows his breath on* ALMA's *fingers.*]

JOHN: I'm a poor excuse for a doctor, I'm much too selfish. But let's try to think about you.

ALMA: Why should you bother about me? [*She sits down*].

150

JOHN: You know I like you and I think you're worth a lot of consideration.

ALMA: Why?

JOHN: Because you have a lot of feeling in your heart, and that's a rare thing. It makes you too easily hurt. Did I hurt you tonight?

ALMA: You hurt me when you sprang up from the sofa and rushed from the rectory in such – in such mad haste that you left your coat behind you!

JOHN: I'll pick up the coat sometime.

ALMA: The time of our last conversation you said you would take me riding in your automobile sometime, but you forgot to.

JOHN: I didn't forget. Many's the time I've looked across at the rectory and wondered if it would be worth trying, you and me ...

ALMA: You decided it wasn't?

JOHN: I went there tonight, but it wasn't you and me ... Fingers warm now?

ALMA: Those tablets work quickly. I'm already feeling drowsy. [*She leans back with her eyes nearly shut.*] I'm beginning to feel almost like a water lily. A water lily on a Chinese lagoon.

[*A heavy iron bell strikes three.*]

ROSA: *Johnny!*

[ALMA *starts to rise.*]

ALMA: I *must* go.

JOHN: I will call for you Saturday night at eight o'clock.

ALMA: What?

JOHN: I'll give you this box of tablets but watch how you take them. Never more than one or two at a time.

ALMA: Didn't you say something else a moment ago?

JOHN: I said I would call for you at the rectory Saturday night.

ALMA: Oh ...

JOHN: Is that all right?

[ALMA *nods speechlessly. She remains with the box nesting in the palm of her hand as if not knowing it was there.* JOHN *gently closes her fingers on the box.*]

ALMA: Oh! [*She laughs faintly.*]

ROSA [*outside*]: *Johnny!*

JOHN: Do you think you can find your way home, Miss Alma?

[ROSA *steps back into the office with a challenging look.* ALMA *catches her breath sharply and goes out of the side door.*

JOHN *reaches above him and turns out the light. He crosses to* ROSA *by the anatomy chart and takes her roughly in his arms. The light lingers on the chart as the interior dims out.*]

SCENE V

In the rectory.
Before the light comes up a soprano voice is heard singing 'From the Land of the Sky Blue Waters'.
As the curtain rises, ALMA *gets up from the piano.* MR *and* MRS WINEMILLER, *also, are in the lighted room.*

ALMA: What time is it, Father?

[MR WINEMILLER *goes on writing. She raises her voice.*]

What time is it, Father?

MR WINEMILLER: Five of eight. I'm working on my sermon.

ALMA: Why don't you work in the study?

MR WINEMILLER: The study is suffocating. So don't disturb me.

ALMA: Would there be any chance of getting Mother upstairs if someone should call?

MR WINEMILLER: Are you expecting a caller?

ALMA: Not expecting. There is just a chance of it.

MR WINEMILLER: Whom are you expecting?

ALMA: I said I wasn't expecting anyone, that there was just. a possibility ...

MR WINEMILLER: Mr Doremus? I thought that this was his evening with his mother?

ALMA: Yes, it is his evening with his mother.

MR WINEMILLER: Then who is coming here, Alma?

ALMA: Probably no one. Probably no one at all.

MR WINEMILLER: This is all very mysterious.

MRS WINEMILLER: That tall boy next door is coming to see her, that's who's coming to see her.

ALMA: If you will go upstairs, Mother, I'll call the drug store and ask them to deliver a pint of fresh peach ice-cream.

MRS WINEMILLER: I'll go upstairs when I'm ready – good and ready, and you can put that in your pipe and smoke it, Miss Winemiller!

[MRS WINEMILLER *lights a cigarette.* MR WINEMILLER *turns slowly away with a profound sigh.*]

ALMA: I may as well tell you who might call, so that if he calls there will not be any unpleasantness about it. Young Dr John Buchanan said he might call.

MRS WINEMILLER: See!

MR WINEMILLER: You can't be serious.

MRS WINEMILLER: Didn't I tell you?

ALMA: Well, I am.

MR WINEMILLER: That young man might come here?

ALMA: He asked me if he might and I said, yes, if he wished to. But it is now after eight so it doesn't look like he's coming.

MR WINEMILLER: If he does come you will go upstairs to your room and I will receive him.

ALMA: If he does come I'll do no such thing, Father.

MR WINEMILLER: You must be out of your mind.

ALMA: I'll receive him myself. You may retire to your study and Mother upstairs. But if he comes I'll receive him. I don't judge people by the tongues of gossips. I happen to know that he has been grossly misjudged and misrepresented by old busy-bodies who're envious of his youth and brilliance and charm!

MR WINEMILLER: If you're not out of your senses, then I'm out of mine.

ALMA: I daresay we're all a bit peculiar, Father . . .

MR WINEMILLER: Well, I have had one almost insufferable cross to bear and perhaps I can bear another. But if you think I'm retiring into my study when this young man comes, probably with a whisky bottle in one hand and a pair of dice in the other, you have another think coming. I'll sit right here and look at him until he leaves. [*He turns back to his sermon.*]

[*A whistle is heard outside the open door.*]

ALMA [*speaking quickly*]: As a matter of fact I think I'll walk down to the drug store and call for the ice-cream myself. [*She crosses to the door, snatching up her hat, gloves and veil.*]

MRS WINEMILLER: There she goes to him! Ha-ha!

    [ALMA *rushes out.*]

MR WINEMILLER [*looking up*]: Alma! Alma!

MRS WINEMILLER: Ha-ha-haaaaa!

MR WINEMILLER: Where is Alma? – Alma! [*He rushes through the door.*] Alma!

MRS WINEMILLER: Ha-ha! Who got fooled? Who got fooled! Ha-haaaa! Insufferable cross yourself, you old – windbag . . .

THE CURTAIN COMES DOWN

SCENE VI

A delicately suggested arbour, enclosing a table and two chairs. Over the table is suspended a torn paper lantern. This tiny set may be placed way downstage in front of the two interiors, which should be darkened out, as in the fountain scenes. In the background, as it is throughout the play, the angel of the fountain is dimly visible.

Music from the nearby pavilion of the casino can be used when suitable for background.

JOHN'*s voice is audible before he and* ALMA *enter.*

JOHN [*from the darkness*]: I don't understand why we can't go in the casino.

ALMA: You do understand. You're just pretending not to.

JOHN: Give me one reason.

ALMA [*coming into the arbour*]: I am a minister's daughter.

JOHN: That's no reason. [*He follows her in. He wears a white linen suit, carrying the coat over his arm.*]

ALMA: You're a doctor. That's a better reason. You can't any more afford to be seen in such places than I can – less!

JOHN [*bellowing*]: Dusty!

DUSTY [*from the darkness*]: Coming!

JOHN: What are you fishing in that pocketbook for?

154

ALMA: Nothing.

JOHN: What have you got there?

ALMA: Let go!

JOHN: Those sleeping tablets I gave you?

ALMA: Yes.

JOHN: What for?

ALMA: I need one.

JOHN: *Now?*

ALMA: Yes.

JOHN: Why?

ALMA: Why? Because I nearly died of heart failure in your auto-mobile. What possessed you to drive like that? A demon?

    [DUSTY *enters*].

JOHN: A bottle of vino rosso.

DUSTY: Sure. [*He withdraws.*]

JOHN: Hey! Tell Shorty I want to hear the 'Yellow Dog Blues'.

ALMA: Please give me back my tablets.

JOHN: You want to turn into a dope-fiend taking this stuff? I said take one when you need one.

ALMA: I need one now.

JOHN: Sit down and stop swallowing air.

    [DUSTY *returns with a tall wine bottle and two thin-stemmed glasses.*]

When does the cock-fight start?

DUSTY: 'Bout ten o'clock, Dr Johnny.

ALMA: When does *what start?*

JOHN: They have a cock-fight here every Saturday night. Ever seen one?

ALMA: Perhaps in some earlier incarnation of mine.

JOHN: When you wore a brass ring in your nose?

ALMA: Then maybe I went to exhibitions like that.

JOHN: You're going to see one tonight.

ALMA: Oh, no, I'm not.

JOHN: That's what we came here for.

ALMA: I didn't think such exhibitions were legal.

JOHN: This is Moon Lake Casino where anything goes.

ALMA: And you're a frequent patron?

JOHN: I'd say constant.

ALMA: Then I'm afraid you must be serious about giving up your medical career.

JOHN: You bet I am. A doctor's life is walled in by sickness and misery and death.

ALMA: I am distressed to hear it. Have you told your father?

JOHN: He won't be told. It was to be – demonstrated.

ALMA: Last night I heard the phone ringing in your office again and again. No one answered. It was agonizing. I shut my bedroom window so that I wouldn't hear it, but I still heard it . . .

JOHN: I heard it too. Screaming at me all night. I haven't answered his phone since he left, Miss Alma. [*He pours wine.*]

ALMA: May I be so presumptuous as to inquire what you'll do when you quit?

JOHN: You may be so presumptuous as to inquire.

ALMA: But you won't tell me?

JOHN: I haven't made up my mind, but I've been thinking of South America lately.

ALMA [*sadly*]: Oh . . .

JOHN: I've heard that cantinas are lots more fun than saloons, and señoritas are caviar among females.

ALMA: Dorothy Sykes' brother went to South America and was never heard of again. It takes a strong character to survive in the tropics. Otherwise its a quagmire.

JOHN: You think my character's weak?

ALMA: I think you're confused, just awfully, awfully confused, as confused as I am – but in a different way . . .

JOHN [*stretching out his legs*]: Hee-haw, ho-hum.

ALMA: You used to say that as a child – to signify your disgust!

JOHN [*grinning*]: Did I?

ALMA [*sharply*]: Don't sit like that!

JOHN: Why not?

ALMA: You look so indolent and worthless.

JOHN: Maybe I am.

ALMA: If you must go somewhere, why don't you choose a place with a bracing climate?

JOHN: Parts of South America are as cool as a cucumber.

ALMA: I never knew that.

JOHN: Well, now you do.

ALMA: Those Latins all dream in the sun – and indulge their senses.

JOHN: Well, it's yet to be proven that anyone on this earth is crowned with so much glory as the one that uses his senses to get all he can in the way of – satisfaction.

ALMA: Self-satisfaction?

JOHN: What other kind is there?

ALMA: I will answer that question by asking you one. Have you ever seen, or looked at a picture of, a Gothic cathedral?

JOHN: Gothic cathedrals? What about them?

ALMA: How everything reaches up, how everything seems to be straining for something out of the reach of stone – or human – fingers? . . . The immense stained windows, the great arched doors that are five or six times the height of the tallest man – the vaulted ceiling and all the delicate spires – all reaching up to something beyond attainment! To me – well, that is the secret, the principle back of existence – the everlasting struggle and aspiration for more than our human limits have placed in our reach . . . Who was that said that – oh, so beautiful thing! – 'All of us are in the gutter, but some of us are looking at the stars!'

JOHN: Mr Oscar Wilde.

ALMA [*somewhat taken aback*]: Well, regardless of who said it, it's still true. Some of us are looking at the stars! [*She looks up raptly and places her hand over his.*]

JOHN: It's no fun holding hands with gloves on, Miss Alma.

ALMA: That's easily remedied. I'll just take the gloves off.

[*Music is heard.*]

JOHN: Christ! [*He rises abruptly and lights a cigarette.*] Rosa Gonzales is dancing in the Casino.

ALMA: You *are* unhappy. You hate me for depriving you of the company inside. Well, you'll escape by and by. You'll drive me home and come back out by yourself . . . I've only gone out with three young men at all seriously, and with each one there was a desert between us.

JOHN: What do you mean by a desert?

ALMA: Oh – wide, wide stretches of uninhabitable ground.

JOHN: Maybe you made it that way by being stand-offish.

ALMA: I made quite an effort with one or two of them.

JOHN: What kind of an effort?

ALMA: Oh, I – tried to entertain them the first few times. I would play and sing for them in the rectory parlour.

JOHN: With your father in the next room and the door half open?

ALMA: I don't think that was the trouble.

JOHN: What was the trouble?

ALMA: I – I didn't have my heart in it. [*She laughs uncertainly.*] A silence would fall between us. You know, a silence?

JOHN: Yes, I know a silence.

ALMA: I'd try to talk and he'd try to talk and neither would make a go of it.

JOHN: The silence would fall?

ALMA: Yes, the enormous silence.

JOHN: Then you'd go back to the piano?

ALMA: I'd twist my ring. Sometimes I twisted it so hard that the band cut my finger! He'd glance at his watch and we'd both know that the useless undertaking had come to a close . . .

JOHN: You'd call it quits?

ALMA: Quits is – what we'd call it . . . One or two times I was rather sorry about.

JOHN: But you didn't have your heart in it?

ALMA: None of them really engaged my serious feelings.

JOHN: You do have serious feelings – of that kind?

ALMA: Doesn't everyone – sometimes?

JOHN: Some women are cold. Some women are what is called frigid.

ALMA: Do I give that impression!

JOHN: Under the surface you have a lot of excitement, a great deal more than any other woman I have met. So much that you have to carry these sleeping pills with you. The question is why? [*He leans over and lifts her veil.*]

ALMA: What are you doing that for?

JOHN: So that I won't get your veil in my mouth when I kiss you.

ALMA [*faintly*]: Do you want to do that?

JOHN [*gently*]: Miss Alma. [*He takes her arms and draws her to her feet.*] Oh, Miss Alma, Miss Alma! [*He kisses her.*]

ALMA [*in a low, shaken voice*]: Not 'Miss' any more. Just Alma.

JOHN [*grinning gently*]: 'Miss' suits you better, Miss Alma.

[JOHN *kisses* ALMA *again. She hesitantly touches his shoulders, but not quite to push him away. He speaks softly to her.*]

Is it so hard to forget you're a preacher's daughter?

ALMA: There is no reason for me to forget that I am a minister's daughter. A minister's daughter's no different from any other young lady who tries to remember that she *is* a lady.

JOHN: This lady stuff, is that so important?

ALMA: Not to the sort of girls that you may be used to bringing to Moon Lake Casino. But suppose that some day ... [*she crosses out of the arbour and faces away from him*] suppose that some day you – married ... The woman that you selected to be your wife, and not only your wife but – the mother of your children! [*She catches her breath at the thought.*] Wouldn't you want that woman to be a lady? Wouldn't you want her to be somebody that you, as her husband, and they as her precious children – could look up to with very deep respect?

[*There is a pause.*]

JOHN: There's other things between a man and a woman besides respect. Did you know that, Miss Alma?

ALMA: Yes ...

JOHN: There's such a thing as intimate relations.

ALMA: Thank you for telling me that. So plainly.

JOHN: It may strike you as unpleasant. But it does have a good deal to do with – connubial felicity, as you'd call it. There are some women that just give in to a man as a sort of obligation imposed on them by the – cruelty of nature! [*He finishes his glass and pours another.*] And there you are.

ALMA: There *I* am?

JOHN: I'm speaking generally.

ALMA: Oh.

[*Hoarse shouts go up from the Casino.*]

JOHN: The cock-fight has started!

ALMA: Since you have spoken so plainly, I'll speak plainly, too. There are some women who turn a possibly beautiful thing into something no better than the coupling of beasts! – but love is what you bring to it.

JOHN: You're right about that.

ALMA: Some people bring just their bodies. But there are some people, there are some women, John – who can bring their hearts to it, also – who can bring their souls to it!

JOHN [*derisively*]: Souls again, huh? – those Gothic cathedrals you dream of!

[*There is another hoarse prolonged shout from the Casino.*]

Your name is Alma and Alma is Spanish for soul. Sometime I'd like to show you a chart of the human anatomy that I have in the office. It shows what our insides are like, and maybe you can show me where the beautiful soul is located on the chart. [*He drains the wine bottle.*] Let's go watch the cock-fight.

ALMA: No!

[*There is a pause.*]

JOHN: I know something else we could do. There are rooms above the Casino . . .

ALMA [*her back stiffening*]: I'd heard that you made suggestions like that to girls that you go out with, but I refused to believe such stories were true. What made you think I might be amenable to such a suggestion?

JOHN: I counted your pulse in the office the night you ran out because you weren't able to sleep.

ALMA: The night I was ill and went to your father for help.

JOHN: It was me you went to.

ALMA: It was your father, and you wouldn't call your father.

JOHN: Fingers frozen stiff when I . . .

ALMA [*rising*]: Oh! I want to go home. But I won't go with you. I will go in a taxi! [*She wheels about hysterically.*] Boy! Boy! Call a taxi!

JOHN: I'll call one for you, Miss Alma. – Taxi! Taxi!

[*He goes out of the arbour.*]

ALMA [*wildly*]: *You're not a gentleman!*

JOHN [*from the darkness*]: Taxi!

ALMA: *You're not a gentleman!*

    [*As he disappears she makes a sound in her throat like a hurt animal. The light fades out of the arbour and comes up more distinctly on the stone angel of the fountain.*]

JOHN [*off*]: Taxi!

END OF PART ONE

PART TWO: A WINTER

The sky and the southern constellations, almost imperceptibly moving with the earth's motion, appear on the great cyclorama.

The rectory interior is lighted first disclosing ALMA *and* ROGER DOREMUS *seated on the green plush sofa under the romantic landscape in its heavy gilt frame. On a tiny table beside them is a cut-glass pitcher of lemonade with cherries and orange slices in it, like a little aquarium of tropical fish.* ROGER *is entertaining* ALMA *with a collection of photographs and postcards, mementoes of his mother's trip to the Orient. He is enthusiastic about them and describes them in phrases his mother must have assimilated from a sedulous study of literature provided by Cook's Tours.* ALMA *is less enthusiastic; she is preoccupied with the sounds of a wild party going on next door at the doctor's home. At present there is Mexican music with shouts and stamping.*

Only the immediate area of the sofa is clearly lighted; the fountain is faintly etched in light and the night sky walls the interior.

ROGER: And this is Ceylon, the Pearl of the Orient!

ALMA: And who is this fat young lady?

ROGER: That is Mother in a hunting costume.

ALMA: The hunting costume makes her figure seem bulky. What was your mother hunting?

ROGER [*gaily*]: Heaven knows what she was hunting! But she found Papa.

ALMA: Oh, she met your father on this Oriental tour?

ROGER: Ha-ha! – yes ... He was returning from India with dysentery and they met on the boat.

ALMA [*distastefully*]: Oh ...

ROGER: And here she is on top of a ruined temple!

ALMA: How did she get up there?

ROGER: Climbed up, I suppose.

ALMA: What an active woman.

ROGER: Oh yes, active – is no word for it! Here she is on an elephant's back in Burma.

ALMA: Ah!

ROGER: You're looking at it upside down, Miss Alma!

ALMA: Deliberately – to tease you.

[*The doorbell rings.*]

Perhaps that's your mother coming to fetch you home.

ROGER: It's only ten-fifteen. I never leave till ten-thirty.

[MRS BASSETT *comes in.*]

ALMA: Mrs Bassett!

MRS BASSETT: I was just wondering who I could turn to when I saw the rectory light and I thought to myself, Grace Bassett, you trot yourself right over there and talk to Mr Winemiller!

ALMA: Father has retired.

MRS BASSETT: Oh, what a pity. [*She sees* ROGER.] Hello, Roger! . . . I saw that fall your mother took this morning. I saw her come skipping out of the Delta Planters' Bank and I thought to myself, now isn't that remarkable, a woman of her age and weight so light on her feet? And just at that very moment – *down she went!* I swear to goodness I thought she had broken her hip! Was she bruised much?

ROGER: Just shaken up, Mrs Bassett.

MRS BASSETT: Oh, how lucky! She certainly must be made out of India rubber! [*She turns to Alma.*] Alma – Alma, if it is not too late for human intervention, your father's the one right person to call up old Dr Buchanan at the fever clinic at Lyon and let him know!

ALMA: About – what?

MRS BASSETT: You must be stone-deaf if you haven't noticed what's been going on next door since the old doctor left to fight the epidemic. One continual orgy!

ALMA: These people who clouded his name outside have come indoors.

MRS BASSETT: Well, not five minutes ago a friend of mine who works at the County Courthouse called to inform me that young Dr John and Rosa Gonzales have taken a licence out and are going to be married tomorrow!

ALMA: Are you – quite certain?

MRS BASSETT: Certain? I'm always certain before I speak!

ALMA: Why would he – do such a thing?

MRS BASSETT: August madness! They say it has something to do with the falling stars. Of course, it might also have something to do with the fact that he lost two or three thousand dollars at the casino which he can't pay except by giving himself to Gonzales' daughter. [*She turns to* ALMA.] Alma, what are you doing with that picture puzzle?

ALMA [*with a faint, hysterical laugh*]: The pieces don't fit!

MRS BASSETT [*to* ROGER]: I shouldn't have opened my mouth.

ALMA: Will both of you please go!

[ROGER *goes out.*]

MRS BASSETT: I knew this was going to upset you. Good night, Alma.

[MRS BASSETT *leaves. Flamenco music is heard from the doctor's house, stamping and hand clapping. The lights come up in his office, where the phone is ringing.* JOHN *enters and stares at the phone, a magnum of champagne in his hand. The ring is repeated again and again.*

ALMA, *in the rectory, crosses to her telephone.*]

ALMA: Long distance, please . . . Please get me the fever clinic at Lyon . . . I want to speak to Dr Buchanan, Senior.

[*In the opposite interior* JOHN *reaches for the phone. But* ROSA, *entering behind him, intercepts him and holds the receiver down with her jewelled fingers.*]

JOHN: You don't think I ought to answer this 'frantic appeal'?

ROSA: No frantic appeal except mine.

[ROSA *leans back across the desk. Music. Torrid embrace. Rectory dims out completely. John's phone rings again.* ROSA *keeps her hand on it.*

JOHN: Maybe someone is bleeding.

ROSA: *You* are bleeding. A little. There is blood on your face.

JOHN: Whenever I leave you I have a little blood on me. You never make love without biting or scratching a little. Why is that?

ROSA: — Because I know I can't hold you.

JOHN: You're doing a better job of it than anyone else. A lot better than Father and his flock of grey people.

ROSA: I hold you for one summer.

[*Guitar: Flamenco. Quick transition.*]

There, now, they play the flamenco! Olé! Olé!

JOHN: Olé! Dance, Rosa!

ROSA [*ecstatically*]: I will dance if you hold your eyes on my body as if your eyes are your hands!

JOHN: I have my eyes on your body.

[ROSA *dances slowly about* JOHN.]

ROSA: Tomorrow we leave here together?

JOHN: Yes, we make a 'voy-age'! — We sail out of Galveston. I have the tickets.

ROSA: Two pieces of paper that you can tear in two.

JOHN: No, we make a vay-aaaage! How do you say it in Spanish?

ROSA: *Viaggio!*

JOHN: *Viaggio!* — over the Gulf, and under the little islands and still further south, and further and further and further, until at night we can see the gold cross in the sky . . .

ROSA: And then what happens?

JOHN: Oh, then we stop. We stop at some — tropical port — to pick up a letter.

ROSA: What letter, Johnny, a letter saying 'Come home'?

JOHN: No. A letter containing a fat cheque from Papa Gonzales.

ROSA: Oh, from Papa?

JOHN: Yes, we'll live on that fat remittance of your papa. Sure. What else? Not long ago that idea would have disgusted me. But something this summer has made it acceptable to me, and not just acceptable. No, more than that. — Necessary! — Has anyone ever slid downhill as fast as I have this summer? Like a greased pig! And yet every evening I put on a clean white suit. I have a dozen. Six in the closet, five in the wash, and one on me! And when I shave in the morning, I don't see a sign of depravity in my face. But all this summer I've spent the days remembering the nights, and anticipating the next one.

[*The phone rings again.* JOHN *stares at it as* ROSA *takes the receiver off the hook.*]

– Dance, Rosa! Why don't you dance?

[ROSA *starts to dance. Suddenly weeping, she throws herself to the floor beside* JOHN.]

ROSA: I can't dance any more.

[*The voice of* GONZALES *is heard, bellowing, in the next room.*]

GONZALES: *The sky is the limit!*

[JOHN *is sobered.*]

JOHN: Why does your father want me for a son-in-law?

ROSA [*sobbing*]: *I want you – I, I want you!*

JOHN [*raising her from the floor*]: Why do you?

ROSA [*clinging to him*]: Maybe because – I was born in Piedras Negras, and grew up in a one-room house with a dirt floor, and all of us had to sleep in that one room, five Mexicans and three geese and a little game-cock named Pepe! Ha-ha! [*She laughs hysterically.*] Pepe was a good fighter! That's how Papa began to make money, winning bets on Pepe! Ha-ha! We all slept in the one room. And in the night, I would hear the love-making. Papa would grunt like a pig to show his passion. I thought to myself, how dirty it was, love making, and how dirty it was to be Mexicans and all have to sleep in one room with a dirt floor and not smell good because there was not any bathtub!

[*The accordion continues.*]

JOHN: What has that got to do with . . . ?

ROSA: Me wanting you? You're tall! You smell good! And, oh, I'm so glad that you never grunt like a pig to show your passion! [*She embraces him convulsively.*] Ah, but *quien sabe*! Something might happen tonight, and I'll wind up with some dark little friend of Papa's.

GONZALES [*imperiously*]: Rosa! Rosa!

ROSA: Si, si, Papa, aqui estoy!

GONZALES [*entering unsteadily*]: The gold beads . . . [*He fingers a necklace of gold beads that* ROSA *is wearing.*] Johnny . . . [*He staggers up*

to JOHN *and catches him in a drunken embrace.*] Listen! When my girl
Rosa was little she see a string a gold bead and she want those gold
bead so bad that she cry all night for it. I don' have money to buy a
string a gold bead so next day I go for a ride up to Eagle Pass and I
walk in a dry good store and I say to the man: 'Please give me a
string a gold bead.' He say: 'Show me the money,' and I say: 'Here
is the money!' And I reach down to my belt and I pull out – not the
money – but this! [*He pulls out a revolver.*] Now – now I have
money, but I still have this! [*Laughing.*] She got the gold bead.
Anything that she want I get for her with this [*he pulls out a roll of
bills*] or this! [*He waves the revolver.*]

JOHN [*pushing* GONZALES *away*]: Keep your stinking breath out of
my face, Gonzales!

ROSA: Dejalo, dejalo, Papa!

GONZALES [*moving unsteadily to the couch, with* ROSA *supporting him*]:
Le doy la tierra y si la tierra no basta – le doy el cielo! [*He collapses on
to the couch.*] The sky is the limit!

ROSA [*to* JOHN]: Let him stay there. Come on back to the party.

[ROSA *leaves the room.* JOHN *goes over to the window facing the
rectory and looks across. The light comes up in the rectory living-room
as* ALMA *enters, dressed in a robe. She goes to the window and looks
across at the doctor's house. As* ALMA *and* JOHN *stand at the windows
looking towards each other through the darkness music is heard. Slowly,
as if drawn by the music,* JOHN *walks out of his house and crosses over
to the rectory.* ALMA *remains motionless at the window until* JOHN
*enters the room, behind her. The music dies away and there is a murmur
of wind. She slowly turns to face* JOHN.]

JOHN: I took the open door for an invitation. The Gulf wind is
blowing tonight ... cools things off a little. But my head's on
fire ...

[ALMA *says nothing.* JOHN *moves a few steps towards her.*]
The silence?

[ALMA *sinks on to the love seat, closing her eyes.*]
Yes, the enormous silence [*He goes over to her.*] I will go in a minute,
but first I want you to put your hands on my face ... [*He crouches
beside her.*] Eternity and Miss Alma have such cool hands.

[JOHN *buries his face in* ALMA's *lap. The attitude suggests a stone Pietà.* ALMA's *eyes remain closed.*

On the other side of the stage DR BUCHANAN *enters his house and the light builds a little as he looks around in the door of his office. The love-theme music fades out and the Mexican music comes up strongly, with a definitely ominous quality, as* ROSA *enters the office from the other side.*]

ROSA: Johnny! [*She catches sight of* DR BUCHANAN *and checks herself in surprise.*] Oh! I thought you were Johnny! . . . But you are Johnny's father . . . I'm Rosa Gonzales!

DR BUCHANAN: I know who you are. What's going on in my house?

ROSA [*nervously*]: John's giving a party because we're leaving tomorrow. [*Defiantly.*] Yes! Together! I hope you like the idea, but if you don't, it don't matter, because *we* like the idea and my father likes the idea.

DR BUCHANAN: You scum, get out of my house!

GONZALES [*drunkenly, sitting up on the couch*]: The sky is the limit.

[DR BUCHANAN *turns to* GONZALES *and raises his silver-headed cane in a threatening gesture.*]

DR BUCHANAN: Get your − swine out of − my house! [*He strikes* GONZALES *with his cane.*] And you, get out of here, do you hear me? And you there, all of you there, corrupting my home with your drinking and lecherous women.

[*A woman screams off-stage.*]

Get out, get out!

GONZALES [*staggering up from the couch in pain and surprise*]: Aieeeee!

ROSA [*breathlessly, backing against the anatomy chart*]: No! No, Papa!

DR BUCHANAN [*striking at the chest of the bull-like man with his cane*]: Get your swine out, I said! Get them out of my house!

[DR BUCHANAN *repeats the blow. The drunken* GONZALES *roars with pain and surprise. He backs up and reaches under his coat.*]

ROSA [*wildly and despairingly*]: No, no, no, no, no, no!

[ROSA *covers her face against the anatomy chart. A revolver is fired. There is a burst of light. The cane drops. The music stops short. Everything dims out but a spot of light on* ROSA *standing against the anatomy chart with closed eyes and her face twisted like that of a tragic mask.*]

[*Senselessly*] Aaaaaahhhhhh ... Aaaaaahhhhhh ...
[*The theme music is started faintly and light disappears from everything but the wings of the stone angel.*]

SCENE VIII

The doctor's office.
The stone angel is dimly visible above.
JOHN *is seated in a hunched position at the table.* ALMA *enters with a coffee tray. The sounds of a prayer come through the inner door.*

MR WINEMILLER:
'Oh, God, to whom all hearts are open
And from whom no secrets are hid,
Help this, Thy servant, in his hour of need,
And if it be Thy will, O Lord, take him unto Thyself,
Granting him the peace of life everlasting. . . .'

JOHN: What is that mumbo-jumbo your father is spouting in there?

ALMA: A prayer.

JOHN: Tell him to quit. We don't want that worn-out magic.

ALMA: You may not want it, but it's not a question of what you want any more. I've made you some coffee.

JOHN: I don't want any.

ALMA: Lean back and let me wash your face off, John. [*She presses a towel to the red marks on his face.*] It's such a fine face, a fine and sensitive face, a face that has power in it that shouldn't be wasted.

JOHN: Never mind that. [*He pushes her hand away.*]

ALMA: You have to go in to see him.

JOHN: I couldn't. He wouldn't want me.

ALMA: This happened because of his devotion to you.

JOHN: It happened because some meddlesome Mattie called him back here tonight. Who was it did that?

ALMA: I did.

JOHN: It *was* you then!

ALMA: I phoned him at the fever clinic in Lyon as soon as I learned what you were planning to do. I told him to come here and stop it.

JOHN: You brought him here to be shot.

ALMA: You can't put the blame on anything but your weakness.

JOHN: *You* call me weak?

ALMA: Sometimes it takes a tragedy like this to make a weak person strong.

JOHN: You – white-blooded spinster! You so right people, pious pompous mumblers, preachers and preacher's daughters, all muffled up in a lot of worn-out magic! And I was supposed to minister to your neurosis, give you tablets for sleeping and tonics to give you the strength to go on mumbling your worn-out mumbo-jumbo!

ALMA: Call me whatever you want, but don't let your father hear your drunken shouting. [*She tries to break away from him.*]

JOHN: Stay here! I want to look at something. [*He turns her about.*] This chart of anatomy, look!

ALMA: I've seen it before. [*She turns away.*]

JOHN: You've never dared to look at it.

ALMA: Why should I?

JOHN: You're scared to.

ALMA: You must be out of your senses.

JOHN: You talk about weakness but can't even look at a picture of human insides.

ALMA: They're not important.

JOHN: That's your mistake. You think you're stuffed with rose-leaves. Turn around and look at it, it may do you good!

ALMA: How can you behave like this with your father dying and you so . . .

JOHN: Hold still! Now listen here to the anatomy lecture. You see this chart? It's a picture of a – a picture of a – tree – with three birds in it. This top bird is the brain. The bird is hungry. He's hungry for something called Truth. He doesn't get much, he's never satisfied with it, he keeps on shaking his cold and weak little wings and saying: 'Cheep! Cheep!' – This bird underneath is the belly. He's hungry, too, but he's the practical bird, just hungry for food! – And down here's the lowest bird – or maybe, the highest, who knows? – Yes, take a look at him, too; he's hungry, too, hungry as both the others and twice as lonesome! – What's he hungry for? Love! – There they all are on the chart! Three birds, three hungry little birds in one tall, withering tree! – Yes, a withering tree they can't fly out of! – Well – I've fed the birds, I've fed all three of those birds as much as I was able. You've fed none of them, nothing! – Well – maybe the middle bird, the practical one, the belly, a little – watery subsistence. – But love? Or Truth? Nothing – nothing but hand-me-down notions – attitudes – poses! And two of the birds in your tree are going to die of starvation before the tree falls down – or gets blown over! That's what I had to tell you, and – now you can go! The anatomy lecture is over.

ALMA: So that is your high conception of human desires. What you have here is not the anatomy of a beast, but a man. And I – I reject your opinion of where love is, and the kind of truth you believe the brain to be seeking! – There is something not shown on the chart.

JOHN: You mean the part that Alma is Spanish for, do you?

ALMA: Yes, that's not shown on the anatomy chart! But it's there, just the same, yes, there! Somewhere, not seen, but there. And it's *that* that I loved you with – that! Not what you mention! – Yes, did love you with, John, did nearly *die* of when you hurt me!

[JOHN *turns slowly to her and speaks gently.*]

JOHN: I wouldn't have made love to you.

ALMA [*uncomprehendingly*]: What?

JOHN: The night at the casino – I wouldn't have made love to you. Even if you had consented to go upstairs. I couldn't have made love to you.

[ALMA *stares at* JOHN *as if anticipating some unbearable hurt.*]

Yes, yes! Isn't that funny? I'm more afraid of your soul than you're afraid of my body. You'd have been as safe as the angel of the fountain – because I wouldn't feel *decent* enough to touch you ...

MR WINEMILLER [*off*]: Alma!

[MR WINEMILLER *comes in.*]

He's resting more easily now.

ALMA: Oh ...

[ALMA *nods her head.* JOHN *reaches for his coffee cup.*]

It's cold. I'll heat it.

JOHN: It's all right.

MR WINEMILLER: Alma, Dr John wants you.

ALMA: I . . .

MR WINEMILLER: He asked if you would sing for him.

ALMA: I – couldn't – now.

JOHN: Go in and sing to him, Miss Alma!

[MR WINEMILLER *withdraws through the outer door.* ALMA *looks back at* JOHN *hunched over the coffee cup. He doesn't return her look. She passes into the blurred orange space beyond the inner door, leaving it slightly open. After a few moments her voice rises softly within, singing.* JOHN *suddenly rises. He crosses to the door, shoves it slowly open and enters.*]

[*Softly and with deep tenderness*] Father?

[*The light dims out in the house, but lingers on the stone angel.*]

SCENE IX

The cyclorama is the faint blue of a late afternoon in autumn. There is band music – a Sousa march – in the distance. As it grows somewhat louder, ALMA *enters the rectory interior in a dressing-gown and with her hair hanging loose. She looks as if she had been through a long illness, the intensity drained, her pale face listless. She crosses to the window frame, but the parade is not in sight, so she returns weakly to the sofa and sits down, closing her eyes with exhaustion.*

The REV. *and* MRS WINEMILLER *enter the outer door frame of the rectory, a grotesque-looking couple.*

MRS WINEMILLER *has on her plumed hat, at a rakish angle, and a brilliant scarf about her throat. Her face wears a roguish smile that suggests a musical-comedy pirate. One hand holds the minister's arm and with the other she is holding an ice-cream cone.*

MR WINEMILLER: Now you may let go of my arm, if you please! She was on her worst behaviour. Stopped in front of the White Star Pharmacy on Front Street and stood there like a mule; wouldn't budge till I bought her an ice-cream cone. I had it wrapped in tissue paper because she had promised me that she wouldn't eat it until we got home. The moment I gave it to her she tore off the paper and walked home licking it every step of the way! – just – just to humiliate me!

[MRS WINEMILLER *offers* MR WINEMILLER *the half-eaten cone, saying: 'Lick?'*]

No, thank you!

ALMA: Now, now children.

[MR WINEMILLER'*s irritation shifts to* ALMA.]

MR WINEMILLER: Alma! Why don't you get dressed? It hurts me to see you sitting around like this, day in, day out, like an invalid when there is nothing particularly wrong with you. I can't read your mind. You may have had some kind of disappointment, but you must not make it an excuse for acting as if the world had come to an end.

ALMA: I have made the beds and washed the breakfast dishes and phoned the market and sent the laundry out and peeled the potatoes and shelled the peas and set the table for lunch. What more do you want?

MR WINEMILLER [*sharply*]: I want you to either get dressed or stay in your room.

[ALMA *rises indifferently, then her father speaks suddenly.*]

At night you get dressed. Don't you? Yes, I heard you slipping out of the house at two in the morning. And that was not the first time.

ALMA: I don't sleep well. Sometimes I have to get up and walk for a while before I am able to sleep.

MR WINEMILLER: What am I going to tell people who ask about you?

ALMA: Tell them I've changed and you're waiting to see in what way.

[*The band music becomes a little louder.*]

MR WINEMILLER: Are you going to stay like this indefinitely?

ALMA: Not indefinitely, but you may wish that I had.

MR WINEMILLER: Stop twisting that ring! Whenever I look at you you're twisting that ring. Give me that ring! I'm going to take that ring off your finger!

[MR WINEMILLER *catches* ALMA'S *wrist. She breaks roughly away from him.*]

MRS WINEMILLER [*joyfully*]: Fight! Fight!

MR WINEMILLER: Oh, I give up!

ALMA: That's better. [*She suddenly crosses to the window as the band music gets louder.*] Is there a parade in town?

MRS WINEMILLER: Ha-ha – yes! They met him at the station with a great big silver loving-cup!

ALMA: Who? Who did they . . . ?

MRS WINEMILLER: That boy next door, the one you watched all the time!

ALMA: Is that true, Father?

MR WINEMILLER [*unfolding his newspaper*]: Haven't you looked at the papers?

ALMA: No, not lately.

MR WINEMILLER [*wiping his eyeglasses*]: These people are grass-hoppers, just as likely to jump one way as another. He's finished the work his father started, stamped out the fever and gotten all of the glory. Well, that's how it is in this world. Years of devotion and sacrifice are overlooked an' forgotten while some young an' lucky walks off with the honours!

[ALMA *has crossed slowly to the window. The sun brightens and falls in a shaft through the frame.*]

ALMA [*suddenly crying out*]: *There he is!*

[JOHN *appears on ramp upper left. Raises the silver loving-cup over his head in a sort of salute. Spot of light on him as the rectory begins to dim out.*]

ALMA: So much has changed – so – quickly . . .

[JOHN *enters the office, puts the cup down on the desk, looks at it, then starts to take off his coat down right.* NELLIE *enters through the inner door, carrying a book. She bangs the book down on the desk.* JOHN *turns and sees her.*]

JOHN: So *you're* the young lady Miss Burke said was waiting for me!

NELLIE: Yes, I'm the young lady – waiting for you!

JOHN: High heels, feathers, and paint!

NELLIE: Not paint!

JOHN: Natural colour?

NELLIE: Excitement.

JOHN: Over what?

NELLIE: Everything! You! You here! Didn't you see me at the depot?
I shouted and waved my arm off! I'm home for Thanksgiving.

JOHN: From where?

NELLIE: Sophie Newcomb's.

[JOHN *remains staring at* NELLIE, *unbelieving. At last she draws a book from under her arm.*]

Here is that nasty book you gave me last summer when I was
pretending such ignorance of things?

JOHN: Only pretending?

NELLIE: Yes.

[JOHN *ignores the book.* NELLIE *tosses it on the table.*]

. . . Well?

[JOHN *laughs uneasily and sits on the table.*]

Shall I go now, or will you look at my tongue? [*She crosses to him, sticking out her tongue.*]

JOHN: Red as a berry!

NELLIE: Peppermint drops! Will you have one? [*She holds out a bag.*]

JOHN: Thanks.

[NELLIE *giggles as* JOHN *takes one.*]

What's the joke, Nellie?

NELLIE: They make your mouth so sweet!

JOHN: So?

NELLIE: I always take one when I hope to be kissed.

JOHN [*after a pause*]: Suppose I took you up on that?

NELLIE: I'm not scared. Are you?

[JOHN *gives* NELLIE *a quick kiss. She clings to him, raising her hand to press his head against her own. He breaks free after a moment and turns the light back on.*]

JOHN [*considerably impressed*]: Where did you learn such tricks?

NELLIE: I've been away to school. But they didn't teach me to
love.

JOHN: Who are you to be using that long word?

NELLIE: That isn't a long word!

JOHN: No? [*He turns away from her.*] Run along, Nellie, before we get into trouble.

NELLIE: Who's afraid of trouble, you or me?

JOHN: I am. Run along! Hear me?

NELLIE: Oh, I'll go. But I'll be back for Christmas! [*She laughs and runs out.*] So long!

JOHN: So long!

[*He whistles and wipes his forehead with a handkerchief.*]

SCENE X

An afternoon in December. At the fountain in the park. It is very windy. ALMA enters upper left. She looks at the angel, drops on her knees to feel the lettering at its base.

MRS BASSETT enters down left – against the wind – followed by ROSEMARY.

MRS BASSETT [*starts to speak off-stage*]: Such wind, such wind!

ROSEMARY: Why, Miss Alma!

MRS BASSETT: Alma, it's been a coon's age since I've seen you.

ALMA: I saw you at the public library last Monday.

MRS BASSETT: I didn't see *you*.

ALMA: I was not visible. I have what they call 'stack permission'.

ROSEMARY: I must feed the birdies! Here, birdies! [*Opens bag and holds out breadcrumbs.*]

MRS BASSETT: Oh, what's that?

ALMA: I am allowed to browse among the shelves. I was browsing among the shelves when I heard you talking about me with the librarian.

ROSEMARY: Here, birds, here, birds!

ALMA: Mrs Bassett, something you said isn't true. I haven't been going out lately, I haven't been very well, but – I am not – as you put it – 'going the way Mother went'.

ROSEMARY [*off*]: Here, birdies, birdies, birds!

MRS BASSETT: Why, Miss Alma, who ever said that you were!

ALMA: YOU did, Mrs Bassett.

MRS BASSETT: Whatever I said was meant kindly out of genuine – affection and – concern! Oh, Alma, Alma, everybody loves you, nobody in Glorious Hill would speak unkindly of you! You ought to start coming to the little club meetings again, we've missed you so. At the last meeting Vernon read his verse play.

ALMA: Oh. – How was it received?

MRS BASSETT: Maliciously! Spitefully and vindictively torn to pieces like children tear wings off butterflies!

ROSEMARY: Here, birdies!

MRS BASSETT: But Vernon rose above it! There's nothing you can't rise above if you keep your courage!

NELLIE [off]: Merry Christmas! [Laugh.] I said – Merry Christmas!

MRS BASSETT: I see that Ewell girl coming and I don't want to meet her! Rosemary? Shall we go now?

ROSEMARY: We might as well. There's nothing but crows in the square and I'm not going to feed them. All the little birds have blown away. [She goes off down right.]

MRS BASSETT [to ALMA]: Merry Christmas! Merry Christmas!

ALMA [as MRS BASSETT goes]: Merry Christmas! [Goes off down left.]
    [NELLIE enters down left.]

NELLIE: Miss Alma! Oh, there you are!

ALMA: Why, Nellie ... Nellie Ewell!

NELLIE: I was by the rectory. Just popped in for a second; the holidays are so short that every minute is precious. They told me you'd gone to the park.

ALMA: This is the first walk I've taken in quite a while.

NELLIE: You've been ill!

ALMA: Not ill, just not very well. How you've grown up, Nellie.

NELLIE: It's just my clothes. Since I went off to Sophie Newcomb, I've picked out my own clothes, Miss Alma. When Mother had jurisdiction over my wardrobe, she tried to keep me looking like a child!

ALMA: Your voice is grown-up, too.

NELLIE: They're teaching me diction, Miss Alma. I'm learning to talk like you, long A's and everything, such as 'cahn't' and 'bahth' and 'lahf' instead of 'laugh'. Yesterday I slipped. I said I 'lahfed and lahfed till I nearly died laughing'. Johnny was so amused at me!

ALMA: Johnny?

NELLIE: Your next-door neighbour!

ALMA: Oh! I'm sure it must be a very fashionable school.

NELLIE: Oh yes, they're preparing us to be young ladies in society. What a pity there's no society here to be a young lady in ... at least not for me, with Mother's reputation!

ALMA: You'll find other fields to conquer.

NELLIE: What's this I hear about *you*?

ALMA: I have no idea, Nellie.

NELLIE: That you've quit teaching singing and gone into retirement.

ALMA: Naturally I had to stop teaching while I was ill and as for retiring from the world ... it's more a case of the world retiring from me.

NELLIE: I know somebody whose feelings you've hurt badly.

ALMA: Why, who could that be, Nellie?

NELLIE: Somebody who regards you as an angel!

ALMA: I can't think who might hold me in such esteem.

NELLIE: Somebody who says that you refused to see him.

ALMA: I saw nobody. For several months. The long summer wore me out so.

NELLIE: Well, anyhow, I'm going to give you your present. [*She hands her a small package from the basket.*]

ALMA: Nellie, you shouldn't have given me anything.

NELLIE: I'd like to know why not?

ALMA: I didn't expect it.

NELLIE: After the trouble you took with my horrible voice?

ALMA: It's very sweet of you, Nellie.

NELLIE: Open it!

ALMA: Now?

NELLIE: Why, sure.

ALMA: It's so prettily wrapped I hate to undo it.

NELLIE: I love to wrap presents and since it was for you, I did a specially dainty job of it.

ALMA [*winding the ribbon about her fingers*]: I'm going to save this ribbon. I'm going to keep this lovely paper too, with the silver stars on it. And the sprig of holly ...

NELLIE: Let me pin it on your jacket, Alma.

ALMA: Yes, do. I hardly realized that Christmas was coming ... [*She unfolds the paper, revealing a lace handkerchief and a card.*] What an exquisite handkerchief.

[*Card drops to the floor.*]

NELLIE: I hate to give people handkerchiefs, it's so unimaginative.

ALMA: I love to get them.

NELLIE: It comes from Maison Blanche!

ALMA: Oh, does it really?

NELLIE: Smell it!

ALMA: Sachet *Roses*! Well, I'm just more touched and pleased than I can possibly tell you!

NELLIE: The card!

NELLIE: You dropped it. [*She snatches up the card and hands it to* ALMA.]

ALMA: Oh, how clumsy of me! Thank you, Nellie. 'Joyeux Noël ... to Alma ... from Nellie and ... [*She looks up slowly.*] John?'

NELLIE: He helped me wrap presents last night and when we came to yours we started talking about you. Your ears must have burned!

[*The wind blows loudly.* ALMA *bends stiffly forward.*]

ALMA: You mean you – spoke well of me?

NELLIE: 'Well of'! We raved, simply raved! Oh, he told me the influence you'd had on him!

ALMA: Influence?

NELLIE: He told me about the wonderful talks he'd had with you last summer when he was so mixed up and how you inspired him and you more than anyone else was responsible for his pulling himself together, after his father was killed, and he told me about ...

[ALMA *rises stiffly from the bench.*]

Where are you going, Miss Alma?

ALMA: To drink at the fountain.

NELLIE: He told me about how you came in the house that night like an angel of mercy!

ALMA [*laughing harshly by the fountain*]: This is the only angel in

Glorious Hill. [*She bends to drink.*] Her body is stone and her blood is mineral water.

[*The wind is louder.*]

NELLIE: How penetrating the wind is!

ALMA: I'm going home, Nellie. You run along and deliver your presents now ... [*She starts away.*]

NELLIE: But wait till I've told you the wonderfullest thing I ...

ALMA: I'm going home now. Good-bye.

NELLIE: Oh – Good-bye, Miss Alma. [*She snatches up her festive basket and rushes in the other direction with a shrill giggle as the wind pulls at her skirt.*]

THE LIGHTS DIM OUT

SCENE XI

An hour later. In JOHN's *office.*

The interior is framed by the traceries of Victorian architecture and there is one irregular section of wall supporting the anatomy chart. Otherwise the stage is open to the cyclorama.

In the background mellow golden light touches the vane of a steeple [a gilded weathercock]. Also the wings of the stone angel. A singing wind rises and falls throughout the scene.

JOHN *is seated at a white enamelled table examining a slide through a microscope.*

A bell tolls the hour of five as ALMA *comes hesitantly in. She wears a russet suit and a matching hat with a plume. The light changes, the sun disappearing behind a cloud, fading from the steeple and the stone angel till the bell stops tolling. Then it brighten again.*

ALMA: No greetings? No greetings at all?

JOHN: Hello, Miss Alma.

ALMA [*speaking with animation to control her panic.*]: How white it is here, such glacial brilliance! [*She covers her eyes, laughing.*]

JOHN: New equipment.

ALMA: Everything new but the chart.

JOHN: The human anatomy's always the same old thing.

ALMA: And such a tiresome one! I've been plagued with sore throats.

JOHN: Everyone has here lately. These Southern homes are all improperly heated. Open grates aren't enough.

ALMA: They burn the front of you while your back is freezing!

JOHN: Then you go into another room and get chilled off.

ALMA: Yes, yes, chilled to the bone.

JOHN: But it never gets quite cold enough to convince the damn fools that a furnace is necessary so they go on building without them.

[*There is the sound of wind.*]

ALMA: Such a strange afternoon.

JOHN: Is it? I haven't been out.

ALMA: The Gulf wind is blowing big, white – what do they call them? cumulus? – clouds over! Ha-ha! It seemed determined to take the plume off my hat, like that fox terrier we had once named Jacob snatched the plume off a hat and dashed around and around the back yard with it like a trophy!

JOHN: I remember Jacob. What happened to him?

ALMA: Oh, Jacob. Jacob was such a mischievous thief. We had to send him out to some friends in the country. Yes, he ended his days as – a country squire! The tales of his exploits ...

JOHN: Sit down, Miss Alma.

ALMA: If I'm disturbing you ...?

JOHN: No – I called the rectory when I heard you were sick. Your father told me you wouldn't see a doctor.

ALMA: I needed a rest, that was all ... You were out of town mostly ...

JOHN: I was mostly in Lyon, finishing up Dad's work in the fever clinic.

ALMA: Covering yourself with sudden glory!

JOHN: Redeeming myself with good works.

ALMA: It's rather late to tell you how happy I am, and also how proud. I almost feel as your father might have felt – if ... And – are you – happy now, John?

JOHN [*uncomfortably, not looking at her*]: I've settled with life on fairly acceptable terms. Isn't that all a reasonable person can ask for?

ALMA: He can ask for much more than that. He can ask for the coming true of his most improbable dreams.

JOHN: It's best not to ask for too much.

ALMA: I disagree with you. I say, ask for all, but be prepared to get nothing! [*She springs up and crosses to the window. She continues.*] No, I haven't been well. I've thought many times of something you told me last summer, that I have a *doppelganger*. I looked that up and I found that it means another person inside me, another self, and I don't know whether to thank you or not for making me conscious of it! — I haven't been well ... For a while I thought I was dying, that that was the change that was coming.

JOHN: When did you have that feeling?

ALMA: August. September. But now the Gulf wind has blown that feeling away like a cloud of smoke, and I know now I'm not dying, that it isn't going to turn out to be that simple ...

JOHN: Have you been anxious about your heart again? [*He retreats to a professional manner and takes out a silver watch, putting his fingers on her wrist.*]

ALMA: And now the stethoscope?

[JOHN *removes the stethoscope from the table and starts to loosen* ALMA's *jacket. She looks down at his bent head. Slowly, involuntarily, her gloved hands lift and descend on the crown of his head. He gets up awkwardly. She suddenly leans towards him and presses her mouth to his.*]

Why don't you say something? Has the cat got your tongue?

JOHN: Miss Alma, what can I say?

ALMA: You've gone back to calling me 'Miss Alma' again.

JOHN: We never really got past that point with each other.

ALMA: Oh, yes, we did. We were so close that we almost breathed together!

JOHN [*with embarrassment*]: I didn't know that.

ALMA: No? Well, I did, I knew it. [*Her hand touches his face tenderly.*] You shave more carefully now? You don't have those little razor cuts on your chin that you dusted with gardenia talcum ...

JOHN: I shave more carefully now.

ALMA: So that explains it!

[ALMA's *fingers remain on his face, moving gently up and down it like a blind person reading Braille. He is intensely embarrassed and gently removes her hands from him.*]

Is it – impossible now?

JOHN: I don't think I know what you mean.

ALMA: You know what I mean, all right! So be honest with me. One time I said 'no' to something. You may remember the time, and all that demented howling from the cock-fight? But now I have changed my mind, or the girl who said 'no', she doesn't exist any more, she died last summer – suffocated in smoke from something on fire inside her. No, she doesn't live now, but she left me her ring – You see? This one you admired, the topaz ring set in pearls ... And she said to me when she slipped this ring on my finger – 'Remember I died empty-handed, and so make sure that your hands have *something in them!*' [*She drops her gloves. She clasps his head again in her hands.*] I said, 'But what about pride?' – She said, 'Forget about pride whenever it stands between you and what you must have!'

[JOHN *takes hold of* ALMA's *wrists.*]

And then I said, 'But what if he doesn't want me?' I don't know what she said then. I'm not sure whether she said anything or not – her lips stopped moving – yes, I think she stopped breathing!

[JOHN *gently removes* ALMA's *craving hands from his face.*]

No?

[JOHN *shakes his head in dumb suffering.*]

Then the answer is 'no'!

JOHN [*forcing himself to speak*]: I have a respect for the truth, and I have a respect for you – so I'd better speak honestly if you want me to speak.

[ALMA *nods slightly.*]

You've won the argument that we had between us.

ALMA: What – argument?

JOHN: The one about the chart.

ALMA: Oh – the chart! [*She turns from him and wanders across to the chart. She gazes up at it with closed eyes, and her hands clasped in front of her.*]

JOHN: It shows that we're not a package of rose leaves, that every interior inch of us is taken up with something ugly and functional and no room seems to be left for anything else in there.

ALMA: No ...

JOHN: But I've come around to your way of thinking, that something else is in there, an immaterial something – as thin as smoke – which all of those ugly machines combine to produce and that's their whole reason for being. It can't be seen so it can't be shown on the chart. But it's there, just the same, and knowing it's there – why, then the whole thing – this – this unfathomable experience of ours – takes on a new value, like some – some wildly romantic work in a laboratory! Don't you see?

[*The wind comes up very loud, almost like a choir of voices. Both of them turn slightly,* ALMA *raising a hand to her plumed head as if she were outdoors.*]

ALMA: Yes, I see! Now that you no longer want it to be otherwise you're willing to believe that a spiritual bond can exist between us two!

JOHN: Can't you believe that I am sincere about it?

ALMA: Maybe you are. But I don't want to be talked to like some incurably sick patient you have to comfort. [*A harsh and strong note comes into her voice.*] Oh, I suppose I am sick, one of those weak and divided people who slip like shadows among you solid strong ones. But sometimes, out of necessity, we shadowy people take on a strength of our own. I have that now. You needn't try to deceive me.

JOHN: I wasn't.

ALMA: You needn't try to comfort me. I haven't come here on any but equal terms. You said, let's talk truthfully. Well, let's do! Unsparingly, truthfully, even shamelessly, then! It's no longer a secret that I love you. It never was. I loved you as long ago as the time I asked you to read the stone angel's name with your fingers. Yes, I remember the long afternoons of our childhood, when I had to stay indoors to practise my music – and heard your playmates calling you, 'Johnny, Johnny!' How it went through me, just to hear your name called! And how I – rushed to the window to watch you jump the porch railing! I stood at a distance, half-way down the block, only to keep in sight of your torn red sweater, racing about the vacant lot you played in. Yes, it had begun that early, this affliction of love, and has never let go of me since, but kept on growing. I've lived next door to you all the days of my life, a weak and divided person who stood in adoring awe of your singleness, of your strength. And that is my story! Now I wish *you* would tell *me* – why didn't it happen between us? Why did I fail? Why did you come almost close enough – and no closer?

JOHN: Whenever we've gotten together, the three or four times that we have . . .

ALMA: As few as that?

JOHN: It's only been three or four times that we've – come face to face. And each of those times – we seemed to be trying to find something in each other without knowing what it was that we wanted to find. It wasn't a body hunger although – I acted as if I thought it might be the night I wasn't a gentleman – at the casino – it wasn't the physical you that I really wanted!

ALMA: I know, you've already . . .

JOHN: You didn't have that to give me.

ALMA: Not at that time.

JOHN: You had something else to give.

ALMA: What did I have?

> [JOHN *strikes a match. Unconsciously he holds his curved palm over the flame of the match to warm it. It is a long kitchen match and it makes a good flame. They both stare at it with a sorrowful understanding that is still perplexed. It is about to burn his fingers.* ALMA *leans forward and blows it out, then she puts on her gloves.*]

JOHN: You couldn't name it and I couldn't recognize it. I thought it was just a Puritanical ice that glittered like flame. But now I believe it *was* flame, mistaken for ice. I still don't understand it, but I know it was there, just as I know that your eyes and your voice are the two most beautiful things I've ever known – and also the warmest, although they don't seem to be set in your body at all . . .

ALMA: You talk as if my body had ceased to exist for you, John, in spite of the fact that you've just counted my pulse. Yes, that's it!

You tried to avoid it, but you've told me plainly. The tables have turned, yes, the tables have turned with a vengeance! You've come around to my old way of thinking and I to yours like two people exchanging a call on each other at the same time, and each one finding the other gone out, the door locked against him and no one to answer the bell! [*She laughs.*] I came here to tell you that being a gentleman doesn't seem so important to me any more, but you're telling me I've got to remain a lady. [*She laughs rather violently.*] The tables have turned with a vengeance! – The air in here smells of ether. – It's making me dizzy ...

JOHN: I'll open a window.

ALMA: Please.

JOHN: There now.

ALMA: Thank you, that's better. Do you remember those little white tablets you gave me? I've used them all up and I'd like to have some more.

JOHN: I'll write the prescription for you. [*He bends to write.*]

[*NELLIE is in the waiting-room. They hear her voice.*]

ALMA: Someone is waiting in the waiting-room, John. One of my vocal pupils. The youngest and prettiest one with the least gift for music. The one that you helped wrap up this handkerchief for me. [*She takes it out and touches her eyes with it.*]

[*The door opens, first a crack. NELLIE peers in and giggles. Then she throws the door wide open with a peal of merry laughter. She has holly pinned on her jacket. She rushes up to JOHN and hugs him with childish squeals.*]

NELLIE: I've been all over town just shouting, shouting!

JOHN: Shouting what?

NELLIE: Glad tidings!

[*JOHN looks at ALMA over NELLIE's shoulder.*]

JOHN: I thought we weren't going to tell anyone for a while.

NELLIE: I couldn't stop myself. [*She wheels about.*] Oh, Alma, has he told *you*?

ALMA [*quietly*]: He didn't need to, Nellie. I guessed ... from the Christmas card with your two names written on it!

[*NELLIE rushes over to ALMA and hugs her. Over NELLIE's shoulder*]

ALMA *looks at* JOHN. *He makes a thwarted gesture as if he wanted to speak. She smiles desperately and shakes her head. She closes her eyes and bites her lips for a moment. Then she releases* NELLIE *with a laugh of exaggerated gaiety.*]

NELLIE: So Alma, you were really the first to know!

ALMA: I'm proud of that, Nellie.

NELLIE: See on my finger! This was the present I couldn't tell you about!

ALMA: Oh, what a lovely, lovely solitaire! But solitaire is such a wrong name for it. Solitaire means single and this means *two*! It's blinding, Nellie! Why, it ... hurts my eyes!

[JOHN *catches* NELLIE'*s arm and pulls her to him. Almost violently* ALMA *lifts her face; it is bathed in tears. She nods gratefully to* JOHN *for releasing her from* NELLIE'*s attention. She picks up her gloves and purse.*]

JOHN: Excuse her, Miss Alma. Nellie's still such a child.

ALMA [*with a breathless laugh*]: I've got to run along now.

JOHN: Don't leave your prescription.

ALMA: Oh, yes, where's my prescription?

JOHN: On the table.

ALMA: I'll take it to the drug store right away!

[NELLIE *struggles to free herself from* JOHN'*s embrace which keeps her from turning to* ALMA.]

NELLIE: Alma, don't go! Johnny, let go of me, Johnny! You're hugging me so tight I can't breathe!

ALMA: Good-bye.

NELLIE: Alma! Alma, you know you're going to sing at the wedding! The very first Sunday in spring! – which will be Palm Sunday! 'The Voice that Breathed o'er Eden.'

[ALMA *has closed the door.* JOHN *shuts his eyes tight with a look of torment. He rains kisses on* NELLIE'*s forehead and throat and lips.*]

THE SCENE DIMS OUT WITH MUSIC

SCENE XII

In the park near the angel of the fountain. About dusk.

ALMA enters the lighted area and goes slowly up to the fountain and bends to drink. Then she removes a small white package from her pocket-book and starts to unwrap it. While she is doing this, a YOUNG MAN comes along. He is dressed in a checked suit and a derby. He pauses by the bench. They glance at each other.

A train whistles in the distance. The YOUNG MAN clears his throat. The train whistle is repeated. The YOUNG MAN crosses towards the fountain, his eyes on ALMA. She hesitates, with the unwrapped package in her hand. Then she crosses towards the bench and stands hesitantly in front of it. He stuffs his hands in his pockets and whistles. He glances with an effect of unconcern back over his shoulder.

ALMA pushes her veil back with an uncertain gesture. His whistle dies out. He sways back and forth on his heels as the train whistles again. He suddenly turns to the fountain and bends to drink. ALMA slips the package back into her purse. As the YOUNG MAN straightens up, she speaks in a barely audible voice.

ALMA: The water – is – cool.

THE YOUNG MAN [*eagerly*]: Did you say something?

ALMA: I said, the water is cool.

THE YOUNG MAN: Yes, it sure is, it's nice and cool!

ALMA: It's always cool.

THE YOUNG MAN: Is it?

ALMA: Yes. Yes, even in summer. It comes from deep underground.

THE YOUNG MAN: That's what keeps it cool.

ALMA: Glorious Hill is famous for its artesian springs.

THE YOUNG MAN: I didn't know that.

> [THE YOUNG MAN *jerkily removes his hands from his pockets.* ALMA *gathers confidence before the awkwardness of his youth.*]

ALMA: Are you a stranger in town?

THE YOUNG MAN: I'm a travelling salesman.

ALMA: Ah, you're a salesman who travels! [*She laughs gently.*] But you're younger than most of them are, and not so fat!

THE YOUNG MAN: I'm just starting out. I travel for Red Goose shoes.

ALMA: Ah! The Delt's your territory?

THE YOUNG MAN: From the Peabody Lobby to Cat-Fish Row in Vicksburg.

[ALMA *leans back and looks at the* YOUNG MAN *under half-closed lids, perhaps a little suggestively.*]

ALMA: The life of a travelling salesman is interesting ... but lonely.

THE YOUNG MAN: You're right about that. Hotel bedrooms are lonely.

[*There is a pause. Far away the train whistles again.*]

ALMA: All rooms are lonely where there is only one person. [*Her eyes fall shut.*]

THE YOUNG MAN [*gently*]: You're tired, aren't you?

ALMA: I? Tired? [*She starts to deny it; then laughs faintly and confesses the truth.*] Yes ... a little ... But I shall rest now. I've just now taken one of my sleeping tablets.

THE YOUNG MAN: So early?

ALMA: Oh, it won't put me to sleep. It will just quiet my nerves.

THE YOUNG MAN: What are you nervous about?

ALMA: I won an argument this afternoon.

THE YOUNG MAN: That's nothing to be nervous over. You ought to be nervous if you *lost* one.

ALMA: It wasn't the argument that I wanted to win ...

THE YOUNG MAN: Well, I'm nervous too.

ALMA: What over?

THE YOUNG MAN: It's my first job and I'm scared of not making good.

[*That mysterious sudden intimacy that sometimes occurs between strangers more completely than old friends or lovers moves them both.* ALMA *hands the package of tablets to him.*]

ALMA: Then you must take one of my tablets.

THE YOUNG MAN: Shall I?

ALMA: Please take one!

THE YOUNG MAN: Yes, I shall.

ALMA: You'll be surprised how infinitely merciful they are. The prescription number is 96814. I think of it as the telephone number of God!

[*They both laugh. He places one of the tablets on his tongue and crosses to the fountain to wash it down.*]

THE YOUNG MAN [*to the stone figure*]: Thanks, angel. [*He gives her a little salute, and crosses back to* ALMA.]

ALMA: Life is full of little mercies like that, not *big* mercies but comfortable *little* mercies. And so we are able to go on. [*She has leaned back with half-closed eyes.*]

THE YOUNG MAN [*returning*]: You're falling asleep.

ALMA: Oh no I'm not. I'm just closing my eyes. You know what I feel like now? I feel like a water-lily?

THE YOUNG MAN: A water-lily?

ALMA: Yes, I feel like a water-lily on a Chinese lagoon. Won't you sit down?

[*The* YOUNG MAN *does.*]

My name is Alma. Spanish for soul! What's yours?

THE YOUNG MAN: Ha-ha! Mine's Archie Kramer. Mucho gusto, as they say in Spain.

ALMA: Usted habla Español, señor?

THE YOUNG MAN: Un poquito! Usted habla Español, señorita?

ALMA: Me tañbien. Un poquito!

THE YOUNG MAN [*delightedly*]: Ha ... ha ... ha! Sometimes un poquito is plenty!

[ALMA *laughs — in a different way than she has ever laughed before, a little wearily, but quite naturally. The* YOUNG MAN *leans towards her confidently.*]

What's there to do in this town after dark?

ALMA: There's not much to do in this town after dark, but there are resorts on the lake that offer all kinds of after-dark entertainment. There's one called Moon Lake Casino. It's under new management now, but I don't suppose its character has changed.

THE YOUNG MAN: What was its character?

ALMA: Gay, very gay, Mr Kramer ...

THE YOUNG MAN: Then what in hell are we sitting here for? Vamonos!

ALMA: Como, no, señor!

THE YOUNG MAN: Ha-ha-ha! [*He jumps up.*] I'll call a taxi. [*He runs off shouting:* 'Taxi! Taxi!']

> [ALMA *rises from the bench. As she crosses to the fountain the grave mood of the play is reinstated with a phase of music. She faces the stone angel and raises her gloved hand in a sort of valedictory salute. Then she turns slowly about towards the audience with her hand still raised in a gesture of wonder and finality as* ...]

THE CURTAIN FALLS

Contemporary ... Provocative ... Outrageous ...
Prophetic ... Groundbreaking ... Funny ... Disturbing ...
Different ... Moving ... Revolutionary ... Inspiring ...
Subversive ... Life-changing ...

What makes a modern classic?

At Penguin Classics our mission has always been to make the best
books ever written available to everyone. And that also means
constantly redefining and refreshing exactly what makes a 'classic'.
That's where Modern Classics come in. Since 1961 they have been an
organic, ever-growing and ever-evolving list of books from the last
hundred (or so) years that we believe will continue to be read over and
over again.

They could be books that have inspired political dissent, such as
Animal Farm. Some, like *Lolita* or *A Clockwork Orange*, may have
caused shock and outrage. Many have led to great films, from *In Cold
Blood* to *One Flew Over the Cuckoo's Nest*. They have broken down
barriers – whether social, sexual, or, in the case of *Ulysses*, the
boundaries of language itself. And they might – like *Goldfinger* or
Scoop – just be pure classic escapism. Whatever the reason, Penguin
Modern Classics continue to inspire, entertain and enlighten millions
of readers everywhere.

'No publisher has had more influence on reading habits than Penguin'
Independent

'Penguins provided a crash course in world literature'
Guardian

The best books ever written

PENGUIN 🐧 CLASSICS

SINCE 1946

Find out more at www.penguinclassics.com